simply scrumptious

simply scrumptious

martha day

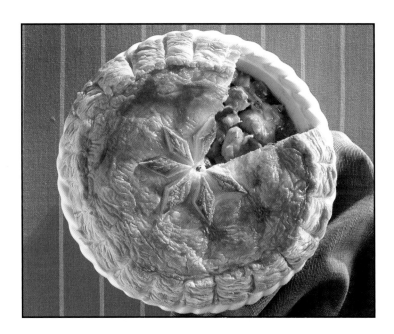

southwater

This edition is published by Southwater

Distributed in the UK by
The Manning Partnership
251–253 London Road East
Batheaston, Bath BA1 7RL
tel. 01225 852 727
fax 01225 852 852

Published in the USA by
Anness Publishing Inc.
27 West 20th Street
Suite 504
New York, NY 10011
fax 212 807 6813

Distributed in Canada by
General Publishing
895 Don Mills Road
400–402 Park Centre
Toronto, Ontario M3C 1W3
tel. 416 445 3333
fax 416 445 5991

Distributed in Australia by
Sandstone Publishing
Unit 1, 360 Norton Street
Leichhardt
New South Wales 2040
tel. 02 9560 7888
fax 02 9560 7488

Publisher Joanna Lorenz
Project Editor Emma Hardy
Designer Lilian Lindblom
Illustrator Anna Koska
Cover photograph Tim Auty
Photographers Karl Adamson, Michael Michaels, James Duncan, Steve Baxter,
Amanda Heywood, Michelle Garrett, Don Last & Patrick McLeavey
Recipes Christine France, Roz Denny, Catherine Atkinson, Liz Trigg, Rosamund Grant,
Sarah Gates, Carole Clements, Elizabeth Wolf-Cohen, Nicola Diggins, Patricia Lousada,
Frances Cleary, Sallie Morris, Shirley Gill & Norma MacMillan

Cover picture shows Florentines. See the recipe on page 60.

For all recipes, quantities are given in both metric and imperial measures, and, where
appropriate, measures are also given in standard cups and spoons. Follow one set, but not
a mixture, because they are not interchangeable.

Previously published as *Home Baking*

1 3 5 7 9 10 8 6 4 2

Contents

Introduction

In an age where so much of what we buy is prepacked, when biscuits come in rolls with tag-pulls for easy opening, freezers are filled with fudge cakes, and ready-to-fill pastry cases are on sale in every supermarket, maybe it is time to campaign for a return to home baking. Remember the smell of newly baked bread, the welcome sight of a batch of fresh scones, the taste of a home-made teabread packed with dried fruits? These are treats few commercial products can match, and if the demands of modern living mean we seldom have time to bake our own biscuits, perhaps we need to look again at how we use the time we have. Baking is one of the most satisfying branches of cookery. Kneading dough can

be very therapeutic after a day dealing with difficult clients or demanding children, and the repetitive task of rolling out dough and cutting out cookies can be positively soothing as an antidote to rush hour travel. Much has been made of the dangers of a diet high in fats and sugars. When you do your own baking, you have far more control over what your family eats. Reducing the amount of refined sugar in cakes and biscuits is easy to achieve, especially if you use dried fruits. Low-fat lunch-box treats, like Apricot Yogurt Cookies on page 58 are a much better bet than chocolate bars.

Home baking doesn't have to be horribly time-consuming. Bread is a cinch thanks to easy-blend yeast, which is added directly to the dry ingredients. You can make the dough in a food processor, if you choose, and as it only needs a single proving, baking a loaf of bread or a dozen rolls is simplicity itself.

Many of the cakes and teabreads in this book take very little time to produce, and even pastry, which some people regard as fiddly, is child's play if you remember a few cardinal rules: when you rub fat into flour, work fast and lift the mixture to incorporate air; add only enough liquid to enable the ingredients to bind together; handle the dough as little as possible and roll it out quickly and lightly. Lining pie plates, spooning in filling and adding pastry lids can take time, especially if you crimp the edges and

decorate the top of the pie, but there's no need to do any of that if you are in a hurry. Just roll out a large circle to fit the pie plate with plenty of overlap, add your filling and lop the extra pastry over. It won't cover the filling completely but that doesn't matter – the rustic effect is part of the charm. The Open Apple Pie on page 95 is made by this method and very good it is too.

For special occasions try some of the more elaborate cakes like the Chocolate Fudge Gâteaux on page 118 or even the Raspberry & Hazelnut Meringue Cake on page 114. Any of these would make a stunning and delicious centrepiece for a celebration tea or a fitting finale to a special dinner party.

Baking Ingredients

SUGAR

Caster sugar is the type most commonly used because it dissolves faster and gives a lighter result. Brown sugar is favoured for its flavour in fruit cakes.

DRIED FRUIT

An invaluable storecupboard ingredient, dried fruit is sold ready-cleaned and seeded for cakes and desserts.

NUTS

Buy nuts only when you need them if possible, as they can become rancid if kept too long. Opened packets can be stored in the fridge or freezer.

BAKING POWDER

Made from bicarbonate of soda, selected acids and starch, this is an effective raising agent, and is added to plain flour.

BICARBONATE OF SODA

This raising agent produces a rapid rise in the presence of an acid. Cakes containing bicarbonate of soda should be baked as soon as possible after mixing.

FLOUR

Most of the recipes in this book use plain, strong or self-raising white flour. Where sifted wholemeal flour is stipulated, return the bran from the sieve to the bowl.

EGGS

Unless recipes specify otherwise, use size 3 eggs. Keep them point-downwards in their box in the fridge, allowing them to come to room temperature before use. Always buy eggs from a reputable supplier.

BUTTER

For rich cakes and pastries, butter is the fat of choice. Two types are available – sweet cream butter and lactic butter, the latter tasting slightly more acidic.

MARGARINE

For most cake mixtures, margarine gives good results. Bring block margarine to room temperature before creaming, but use soft margarine straight from the fridge.

OILS

Choose light oils with no discernible flavour for baking. Sunflower oil is ideal, but groundnut oil or vegetable oil are also fine for most baking purposes.

YEAST

Breads and some cakes use yeast as the raising agent. The development of easy-blend yeast has revolutionized home baking because it is so quick and simple to use, although some cooks still prefer to bake with fresh yeast. A third kind of yeast, active dried yeast, has now largely been replaced by easy-blend yeast.

9

Types of Pastry

FILO

This traditional Greek pastry comes ready rolled in paper-thin sheets, which are layered, then cooked until crisp. Filo is made with very little fat, so each layer must be brushed with oil or melted butter. It dries out quickly when exposed to the air, so any pastry not in use should be kept covered with a clean damp dish towel. Bake the filo pie as soon as it is assembled.

PUFF PASTRY

This delectable pastry is made in such a way that it separates into crisp, melt-in-the-mouth layers when cooked, thanks to air trapped in the pastry. A block of butter is wrapped in a basic dough; the pastry is then turned, rolled, folded and chilled several times. Although some cooks continue to prepare their own puff pastry, many prefer to buy it ready-made and frozen. Thaw slowly (see package instructions).

FLAKY PASTRY

Similar to puff pastry, but easier to prepare, this involves making a dough with half the stipulated amount of butter, then softening the rest to the same consistency as the dough and dotting some of it all over the surface of the rolled out rectangle of pastry. The pastry is folded, turned and rolled and the process repeated. When the pastry is baked in a hot oven it separates into crisp leaves that are beautifully light.

ROUGH PUFF

The easiest flaky pastry of all: the diced fat is mixed with the flour but not rubbed in, so that when the liquid is added a dough is formed in which the fat can be seen. The pastry is rolled and folded several times before being rested and baked. The fat for rough puff pastry should be very cold and it is helpful if the flour is chilled before use.

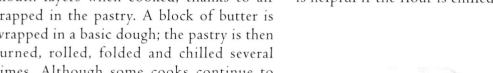

SHORTCRUST

One of the easiest of pastries, shortcrust consists of flour and fat, with just enough liquid to bind the ingredients together. The standard recipe is to sift 175g/6oz/1½ cups plain flour and a pinch of salt into a bowl, then rub in 75g/3oz/6 tbsp diced butter or solid block margarine until it forms fine crumbs. Drizzle 30-45ml/2-3 tbsp iced water over the surface, then quickly fork it through until the pastry clumps together and can be shaped to a ball. If time permits, wrap shortcrust pastry in clear film and chill it for 30 minutes before rolling it out.

RICH SHORTCRUST

Richer than plain shortcrust, this sets to a crisper crust. It is often used for fruit pies. Use the standard shortcrust recipe but make with 115g/4oz/8 tbsp butter and substitute an egg yolk for part of the liquid. For a sweet pastry, add 10–15ml/2–3 tbsp caster sugar after rubbing in the fat.

COOK'S TIPS

To make a quick all-in-one pastry using tub margarine, cream 115g/4oz/ ½ cup tub margarine with 25g/ 1oz/¼ cup plain flour and 15ml/ 1 tbsp cold water. Add a further 150g/ 5oz/ 1¼ cups plain flour and a pinch of salt and work to a smooth dough. Wrap and chill before use.

Make up a batch of rubbed-in mixture for shortcrust pastry (without adding any liquid), put it in a tub and store it in the freezer. Next time you want to make a pie, just thaw, add water and roll out.

If you prefer to use wholemeal flour, but find it makes your pastry rather chewy, use half wholemeal and half plain flour.

Spicy pastry is perfect for apple pie. Make a rich shortcrust, but add 5ml/ 1 tsp each of ground allspice and cinnamon for every 115g/ 4oz/ 1 cup flour.

Baking Techniques

KNEADING

Working yeast dough by folding it towards you, then pushing it down and away with the heel of one or both hands. The dough is turned and the action repeated, often for several minutes, until it feels elastic and no longer sticky.

FOLDING

Lightly mixing an aerated ingredient such as whisked egg whites into other ingredients so that the air does not escape. A metal spoon or a rubber spatula is used with a very light up-and-over action, turning the bowl as you work.

CREAMING

Beating together softened fats with sugar, using a wooden spoon or electric whisk, to make a mixture that resembles whipped cream.

RUBBING-IN

The diced fat (usually butter) is added to the flour, then rubbed between the fingertips until the mixture resembles breadcrumbs.

PROVING

Putting the dough in a covered bowl (or the baking tin), covering and setting aside in a warm place, such as an airing cupboard, until doubled in bulk.

LINING A ROUND TIN

Draw two circles on greaseproof or non-stick baking paper to fit the bottom of the tin and cut out. Then cut a long strip slightly longer than the circumference of the tin and about 5cm/2in taller. Crease the paper strip about 2.5cm/1in from a long side, then snip the paper diagonally at intervals from edge to fold. Grease the tin lightly with oil, fit one of the paper circles in the bottom, then fit the long strip around the inside with the snipped fringe overlapping neatly at the bottom. Brush lightly with oil, then fit the second paper circle in place at the bottom of the tin.

LINING A SQUARE TIN

Cut a piece of greaseproof or non-stick baking paper big enough to cover the bottom of the tin and come up the sides, adding an extra 2.5cm/1in all round. Centre the tin on the paper, then make four cuts in from the side of the paper to the corners of the tin. Overlap the corners of the paper to construct a box the same shape as the tin. Grease the tin and fit the lining in place.

13

TIME-SAVING TIP

Freeze appropriate amounts of rubbed-in mixture. Thaw when needed and use for cakes, pastries or crumble toppings. Add sugar and spice as required.

Breads & Rolls

Nothing is more evocative than the tantalizing aroma of fresh home baking. From aromatic Olive & Oregano Bread to irresistible Clover Leaf Rolls, this chapter includes an enticing selection of the most delicious breads and rolls.

White Bread

INGREDIENTS

25g / 1oz / 2 tbsp butter
475ml / 16fl oz / 2 cups milk
800g / 1¾lb / 7 cups strong white flour
10ml / 2 tsp salt
5ml / 1 tsp caster sugar
15ml / 1 tbsp easy-blend dried yeast
beaten egg, for glazing

MAKES 2 LOAVES

16

1 Melt the butter in the milk in a saucepan. Pour into a jug and cool to hand-hot. Sift the flour into a large mixing bowl and stir in the salt, caster sugar and yeast. Make a well in the centre and add the milk mixture. Mix to a soft dough.

2 Lightly grease two 450g/1lb loaf tins. Knead the dough on a lightly floured surface for about 10 minutes or until it is smooth and elastic. Divide the dough  in half, shape each half into a loaf shape and place in the prepared loaf tins.

3 Slip the tins into a large, lightly oiled plastic bag and leave them to rise in a warm place for about 1 hour or until the loaves have doubled in bulk.

4 Preheat the oven to 200°C/400°F/Gas 6. Glaze the loaves with beaten egg and bake for 40–45 minutes or until well risen and golden brown. Turn out and cool on a wire rack.

Wholemeal Bread

INGREDIENTS

450ml / ¾ pint / 1¾ cups water
30ml / 2 tbsp clear honey
550g / 1lb 5oz / 5¼ cups wholemeal flour
10ml / 2 tsp salt
20ml / 4 tsp easy-blend dried yeast
40g / 1½oz / ¾ cup wheatgerm
45ml / 3 tbsp corn oil
milk, for glazing

MAKES 1 LOAF

1 Heat the water in a small pan to simmering point. Stir in the honey until dissolved. Pour into a jug and cool to hand-hot.

2 Combine the flour, salt, yeast and wheatgerm in a mixing bowl. Make a well in the centre and pour in the oil, with enough liquid to make a soft dough.

3 Lightly grease a 450g/1lb loaf tin. Knead the dough on a lightly floured surface for 10 minutes. Shape into a loaf and place in the prepared tin. Slip the tin into a lightly oiled plastic bag and leave the loaf to rise in a warm place for about 1 hour or until doubled in bulk. Preheat the oven to 200°C/400°F/Gas 6.

4 Glaze the loaf with the milk. Bake for 35–40 minutes until the crust is golden brown. The loaf should sound hollow when rapped underneath. Allow to cool on a wire rack.

17

Multi-grain Bread

INGREDIENTS

65g / 2½oz / generous ¾ cup rolled oats
600ml / 1 pint / 2½ cups milk
60ml / 4 tbsp sunflower oil
60g / 2oz / ⅓ cup soft light brown sugar
30ml / 2 tbsp clear honey
450g / 1lb / 4 cups strong white flour
175g / 6oz / 2 cups soya flour
350g / 12oz / 3 cups wholemeal flour
25g / 1oz / ½ cup wheatgerm
10ml / 2 tsp salt
2 x 10g / ¼oz sachets easy-blend dried yeast
2 eggs, lightly beaten

MAKES 2 LOAVES

I Place the oats in a large bowl. In a saucepan, bring the milk to just below boiling point. Pour the hot milk over the oats, then stir in the oil, sugar and honey.

2 Allow the oat mixture to cool. Combine the flours, wheatgerm, salt and yeast in a large mixing bowl. Add the oat mixture and eggs and mix to a rough dough. Knead on a lightly floured surface for about 10 minutes, until smooth and elastic.

3 Grease two 23 x 13cm/9 x 5in loaf tins. Divide the dough into four equal pieces and roll each to a rope slightly longer than the tin and about 4cm/1½in thick. Twist the ropes together in pairs and place in the tins. Cover loosely and leave to rise in a warm place until doubled in size.

4 Preheat the oven to 220°C/425°F/ Gas 7. Bake the loaves for about 30–35 minutes or until the bottoms of each loaf sound hollow when they are lightly tapped. (Tap the bottoms of both the loaves by clenching your hand together to make a fist and hold the top of the loaf with your other hand.) Cool on a rack.

Rye Bread

INGREDIENTS

475ml/16fl oz/2 cups water
30ml/2 tbsp molasses
350g/12oz/3 cups wholemeal flour
225g/8oz/2 cups rye flour
115g/4oz/1 cup strong white flour
7.5ml/1½ tsp salt
10g/¼oz sachet easy-blend dried yeast
30ml/2 tbsp caraway seeds
30ml/2 tbsp sunflower oil

MAKES 2 LOAVES

1 Heat the water in a small pan to simmering point. Stir in the molasses until dissolved. Pour into a jug and cool to hand-hot.

2 Sift the three types of flour into a large mixing bowl. Stir in the salt and yeast. Set 5ml/1 tsp of the caraway seeds aside and add the rest to the bowl.

3 Make a well in the centre. Then add the oil, with enough of the hand-hot liquid to make a soft dough. Add a little more of the liquid if necessary.

4 Knead the dough on a lightly floured surface for 10 minutes, until smooth and elastic. Divide in half and shape each piece to a 23cm/9in long oval loaf.

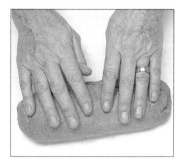

5 Grease a large baking sheet. Put the loaves on the sheet, leaving room for rising. Flatten them slightly. Slide the baking sheet into a lightly oiled large plastic bag and leave in a warm place for up to 2 hours, until the dough has doubled in bulk. Preheat the oven to 200°C/400°F/Gas 6.

6 Brush the loaves with water and sprinkle with the reserved caraway seeds. Bake for 30 minutes or until well risen. The loaves should sound hollow when rapped underneath. Cool on a wire rack.

Cheese Bread

INGREDIENTS

25g / 1oz / 2 tbsp butter
250ml / 8fl oz / 1 cup milk
350g / 12oz / 3 cups strong white flour
10ml / 2 tsp salt
10g / ¼oz sachet easy-blend dried yeast
*115g / 4oz / 1 cup grated mature
Cheddar cheese*

MAKES 1 LOAF

22

1 Melt the butter in the milk in a saucepan. Pour into a jug and cool to hand-hot. Sift the flour into a large mixing bowl and stir in the salt and yeast. Make a well in the centre and add the milk mixture. Mix to a soft dough.

2 Knead the dough on a lightly floured surface for 10 minutes, then pat it flat and sprinkle with the grated Cheddar cheese. Gather up the dough and knead again to distribute the cheese evenly.

3 Lightly grease a loaf tin. Twist the dough, form into a loaf shape and place in the tin, tucking the ends under. Cover loosely and leave in a warm place for about 1 hour, until doubled in bulk.

4 Preheat the oven to 200°C/400°F/Gas 6. Bake the loaf for 15 minutes, then lower the heat to 190°C/375°F/Gas 5 and bake for 20–30 minutes more, or until the bottom sounds hollow when rapped. Cool on a wire rack.

VARIATION
Try this recipe with grated Red Leicester cheese, Gruyère or Jarlsberg for a delicious alternative.

Dill Bread

INGREDIENTS

60ml/4 tbsp olive oil
½ onion, chopped
800–900g/1¾–2lb/7–8 cups strong
white flour
10ml/2 tsp salt
15ml/1 tbsp caster sugar
2 x 10g/¼oz sachets easy-blend dried yeast
1 large bunch dill, finely chopped
2 eggs, lightly beaten
115g/4oz/½ cup cottage cheese
475ml/16fl oz/2 cups hand-hot water
milk, for glazing

MAKES 2 LOAVES

1 Heat 15ml/1 tbsp of the olive oil in a small frying pan and fry the onion until soft. Set aside to cool. Lightly grease a large baking sheet.

2 Combine the flour, salt, sugar and yeast in a large mixing bowl. Make a well in the centre and add the onion (with the cooking oil), dill, eggs, cottage cheese and remaining oil. Stir in enough of the hand-hot water to make a soft dough.

3 Knead the dough on a lightly floured surface until smooth and elastic. Divide in half and shape each piece into a round.

4 Place the rounds of dough on the baking sheet, cover loosely and leave to rise in a warm place for about 1 hour or until doubled in bulk. Preheat the oven to 190°C/375°F/Gas 5.

5 Score the tops of the loaves, glaze with milk and bake for about 45 minutes, until browned. Allow the loaves to cool slightly on a wire rack before serving.

23

Olive & Oregano Bread

INGREDIENTS

15ml / 1 tbsp olive oil
1 onion, finely chopped
450g / 1lb / 4 cups strong white flour, plus
extra for dusting
5ml / 1 tsp salt
1.5ml / ¼ tsp ground black pepper
5ml / 1 tsp easy-blend dried yeast
50g / 2oz / ⅓ cup stoned black olives,
roughly chopped
15ml / 1 tbsp black olive paste
15ml / 1 tbsp chopped fresh oregano
15ml / 1 tbsp chopped fresh parsley
300ml / ½ pint / 1¼ cups hand-hot water

MAKES 1 LOAF

1 Heat the olive oil in a frying pan. Add the onion and fry over a medium heat for 4–5 minutes, until golden. Grease a large baking sheet.

2 Sift the flour and salt into a large mixing bowl. Stir in the pepper and yeast. Make a well in the centre and add the fried onion (with the cooking oil), olives, olive paste and herbs. Stir in enough of the hand-hot water to make a soft dough, adding a little more water if necessary.

3 Transfer the dough to a lightly floured surface and knead for 10 minutes, until smooth and elastic. Shape to a 20cm/8in round and place on the prepared baking sheet.

4 Using a sharp knife, make criss-cross cuts over the top of the dough. Slip the baking sheet into a lightly oiled plastic bag and leave the loaf to rise in a warm place for about 1 hour, until doubled in bulk. Preheat the oven to 220°C/425°F/Gas 7.

5 Dust the loaf with a little flour. Bake for 10 minutes, then lower the oven temperature to 200°C/400°F/Gas 6 and bake for 20 minutes more. The loaf is ready when it sounds hollow when rapped underneath. Cool the loaf slightly on a wire rack. Serve warm.

COOK'S TIP
This bread is delicious served with minestrone or a simple tomato and mozzarella salad.

24

Sage Soda Bread

INGREDIENTS

225g/8oz/2 cups wholemeal flour
115g/4oz/1 cup strong white flour
2.5ml/½ tsp salt
5ml/1 tsp bicarbonate of soda
30ml/2 tbsp shredded fresh sage leaves
300–450ml/½–¾ pint/1¼–1¾
cups buttermilk

MAKES 1 LOAF

1 Preheat the oven to 220°C/425°F/Gas 7. Lightly oil a baking sheet. Sift both types of flour into a bowl, then tip in any bran remaining in the sieve. Stir in the salt, bicarbonate of soda and sage.

2 Add enough of the buttermilk to make a soft dough, mixing just enough to combine the ingredients. Shape the dough into a round and place on the baking sheet.

3 Cut a deep cross in the top of the loaf. Bake for 40 minutes or until the loaf is well risen and sounds hollow when rapped underneath. Cool on a wire rack. Serve warm, with butter.

Courgette Crown Bread

INGREDIENTS

450g / 1lb courgettes
salt
500g / 1¼lb / 5 cups strong white flour
2 x 10g / ¼oz sachets easy-blend dried yeast
50g / 2oz / ⅔ cup grated Parmesan cheese
ground black pepper
30ml / 2 tbsp olive oil
300ml / ½ pint / 1¼ cups hand-hot water
milk, for glazing
sesame seeds, for the topping

MAKES I LOAF

4 Shape the dough into eight rolls. Fit them into the cake tin, brush the tops with the milk and sprinkle with sesame seeds. Allow the dough rolls to rise again.

5 Preheat the oven to 200°C/400°F/Gas 6. Bake the bread for 25 minutes or until golden brown. Cool on a wire rack.

1 Top and tail the courgettes, then grate them into a colander. Sprinkle each layer lightly with salt. Leave to drain for 30 minutes, then rinse, drain and pat dry.

2 Grease and base line a 23cm/9in round sandwich cake tin. Mix the flour, yeast and Parmesan in a large mixing bowl. Season with black pepper.

3 Stir in the oil and courgettes and add enough of the hand-hot water to make a fairly firm dough. Knead on a lightly floured surface for 10 minutes. Return to the clean bowl, cover and leave in a warm place to rise for 1 hour or until doubled in bulk.

Parma Ham & Parmesan Bread

INGREDIENTS

*225g/8oz/2 cups self-raising
wholemeal flour
225g/8oz/2 cups self-raising white flour
5ml/1 tsp baking powder
5ml/1 tsp salt
5ml/1 tsp ground black pepper
75g/3oz Parma ham, chopped
25g/1oz/⅓ cup grated Parmesan cheese
30ml/2 tbsp chopped fresh parsley
45ml/3 tbsp Meaux mustard
350ml/12fl oz/1½ cups buttermilk, plus
extra for glazing*

MAKES I LOAF

1 Preheat the oven to 200°C/400°F/Gas 6. Lightly flour a baking sheet. Place the wholemeal flour in a bowl and sift in the white flour, baking powder and salt. Stir in the pepper and the ham. Set aside about 15ml/1 tbsp of the grated Parmesan and stir the rest into the mixture, with the parsley. Make a well in the centre.

2 Mix the mustard and buttermilk in a jug, pour on to the flour mixture and quickly mix to a soft dough. Knead briefly on a lightly floured surface, then shape the dough into an oval loaf.

3 Brush the loaf with buttermilk, sprinkle with the reserved Parmesan and place on the baking sheet. Bake for 25–30 minutes, or until golden brown. Cool on a wire rack.

COOK'S TIP

If you can't locate buttermilk, use lightly soured milk instead. Stir 5ml/1 tsp lemon juice into 350ml/12fl oz/1½ cups milk. Set aside for 15 minutes before use.

28

Corn Bread

INGREDIENTS

115g/4oz/1 cup plain flour
75g/3oz/6 tbsp caster sugar
5ml/1 tsp salt
15ml/1 tbsp baking powder
175g/6oz/1½ cups cornmeal (polenta)
350ml/12fl oz/1½ cups milk
2 eggs
75g/3oz/6 tbsp butter, melted
115g/4oz/½ cup solid margarine, melted

MAKES 1 LOAF

1 Preheat the oven to 200°C/400°F/Gas 6. Grease a 450g/1lb loaf tin. Line the base with non-stick baking paper.

2 Sift the flour, sugar, salt and baking powder into a large mixing bowl. Stir in the cornmeal. Make a well in the centre of the flour with a wooden spoon.

3 Whisk the milk and eggs with the melted butter and margarine until well combined. Pour the mixture into the well in the flour mixture. Stir until just blended; do not overmix or the cooked bread will not be light.

4 Pour into the prepared tin and bake for about 45 minutes, or until a skewer inserted in the centre of the loaf comes out clean. Turn on to a wire rack. Serve hot or at room temperature. The bread makes an excellent accompaniment to a Mexican meal.

Sesame Seed Bread

INGREDIENTS

175g/6oz/1½ cups plain white flour
175g/6oz/1½ cups wholemeal flour
5ml/1 tsp salt
10ml/2 tsp easy-blend dried yeast
300ml/½ pint/1¼ cups hand-hot water
25g/1oz/½ cup toasted sesame seeds
milk, for glazing
30ml/2 tbsp sesame seeds, for sprinkling

MAKES 1 LOAF

4 Glaze the loaf with the milk. Sprinkle with the sesame seeds. Bake for 15 minutes, then lower the oven temperature to 190°C/375°F/Gas 5 and bake for about 30 minutes more, until the loaf is golden and sounds hollow when rapped underneath. Cool on a wire rack.

1 Sift the flours into a large mixing bowl, then stir in the salt and yeast. Make a well in the centre and stir in enough of the hand-hot water to make a rough dough.

2 Knead the dough on a lightly floured surface for 10 minutes, or until smooth and elastic. Knead in the sesame seeds until evenly distributed.

3 Grease a 23cm/9in cake tin. Divide the dough into 16 balls and fit them side by side in the tin. Cover with a lightly oiled plastic bag and leave in a warm place for about 1 hour, or until the loaf has risen to above the rim of the tin. Preheat the oven to 220°C/425°F/Gas 7.

Poppy Seed Knots

INGREDIENTS

350ml/12fl oz/1½ cups milk
50g/2oz/¼ cup unsalted butter
675g/1½lb/6 cups strong white flour
10ml/2 tsp salt
10g/¼oz sachet easy-blend dried yeast
1 egg yolk
1 egg, to glaze
10ml/2 tsp water
poppy seeds (see method)

MAKES 18

1 Heat the milk and butter in a saucepan, stirring occasionally, until the butter has melted. Pour into a jug and cool to hand-hot.

2 Sift the flour and salt into a bowl. Stir in the yeast. Make a well in the centre and add the milk mixture and the egg yolk. Mix to a soft dough. Knead on a lightly floured surface for about 10 minutes, until smooth and elastic but not sticky.

3 Grease a large baking sheet. Divide the dough into 18 pieces, about the size of golf balls. Roll each piece into a rope and twist to form a knot. Place the knots 2.5cm/1in apart on the baking sheet. Cover loosely and leave to rise in a warm place until the knots have doubled in size.

4 Preheat the oven to 230°C/450°F/ Gas 8. Beat the egg with the water in a cup. Brush the glaze over the knots and sprinkle with the poppy seeds. Bake for 12–15

minutes or until the tops of the knots are lightly browned. Transfer the knots to a rack and leave to cool slightly before serving warm.

Clover Leaf Rolls

INGREDIENTS

300ml / ½ pint / 1 ¼ cups milk
50g / 2oz / ¼ cup unsalted butter
450g-500g / 1-1 ¼lb / 4-5 cups strong
white flour
10ml / 2 tsp salt
30ml / 2 tbsp caster sugar
10g / ¼oz sachet easy-blend dried yeast
1 egg, beaten
melted butter, for glazing

MAKES 24

1 Place the milk and butter in a saucepan and heat, stirring occasionally, until the butter has melted. Pour into a jug and cool to hand-hot.

2 Sift 450g/1lb/ 4 cups of the flour with the salt into a large bowl. Stir in the sugar and yeast. Make a well in the centre, add the milk and butter mixture, then add the beaten egg. Mix to a rough dough, adding more flour if necessary. Knead on a lightly floured surface for about 10 minutes, until the dough is smooth, elastic and no longer sticky.

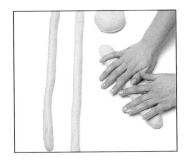

3 Grease two 12-cup bun tins with a small amount of oil. Divide the dough into four equal pieces and, with your hands, roll each piece to a rope about 35cm/ 14in long. Cut each rope into about 18 pieces and form each piece into a small ball.

4 Place three of the balls, side by side, in each bun cup. Cover loosely and leave to rise in a warm place until almost doubled in size. Meanwhile, preheat the oven to 230°C/450°F/Gas 8. Brush the rolls lightly with melted butter to glaze. Bake for about 12–15 minutes or until lightly browned. Cool slightly on a rack before serving.

32

Teabreads, Muffins & Biscuits

Make tea-time a memorable occasion with these irresistible teabreads, muffins and biscuits. Try the deliciously light Lemon and Walnut Teabread or the mouth watering Dried Cherry Muffins. You're sure to find a real treat for everyone.

Lemon & Walnut Teabread

INGREDIENTS

115g/4oz/½ cup butter or margarine, at room temperature
115g/4oz/½ cup granulated sugar
2 eggs, separated
grated rind of 2 lemons
30ml/2 tbsp lemon juice
225g/8oz/2 cups plain flour
10ml/2 tsp baking powder
120–150ml/4–5fl oz/½–⅔ cup milk
50g/2oz/½ cup chopped walnuts
pinch of salt

MAKES 1 LOAF

1 Preheat the oven to 180°C/350°F/Gas 4. Grease a 450g/1lb loaf tin and base line it with non-stick baking paper.

2 Cream the butter or margarine with the sugar until light and fluffy. Beat in the egg yolks, then stir in the lemon rind and juice.

3 In another bowl, sift the flour and baking powder together three times. Fold into the creamed mixture in three batches, alternating with 120ml/4fl oz/½ cup of the milk. Fold in the walnuts. The mixture should be quite stiff; add the extra milk only if absolutely necessary.

4 Whisk the egg whites with the salt in a bowl until stiff. Fold half the egg white into the walnut mixture to lighten it, then fold in the rest until just mixed.

5 Spoon the mixture into the prepared tin. Bake for 45 minutes or until a thin skewer inserted in the teabread comes out clean. Cool on a wire rack.

Pineapple & Apricot Teabread

INGREDIENTS

225g/8oz/2 cups plain flour
1.5ml/¼ tsp salt
7.5ml/1½ tsp baking powder
175g/6oz/¾ cup unsalted butter
150g/5oz/⅔ cup caster sugar
3 eggs, beaten
few drops of vanilla essence
115g/4oz/⅔ cup crystallized pineapple, chopped
115g/4oz/⅔ cup crystallized ginger, chopped
225g/8oz/1⅓ cups ready-to-eat dried apricots, chopped
grated rind and juice of ½ orange
grated rind and juice of ½ lemon
milk (see method)

MAKES 1 LOAF

1 Preheat the oven to 180°C/350°F/Gas 4. Line an 18cm/7in square cake tin with greaseproof paper. Grease the paper. Sift the flour, salt and baking powder into a bowl.

2 Cream the butter and sugar together in a mixing bowl until pale and fluffy. Gradually add the beaten eggs, beating well after each addition, and adding a little of the flour mixture if the mixture shows signs of curdling. Beat in the vanilla essence, then fold in half of the remaining flour mixture.

3 Fold in the pineapple, ginger, apricots and grated citrus rind, with the rest of the flour. Add enough of the citrus juice to give a fairly soft dropping consistency. (Add a little milk if necessary). Spoon into the prepared tin and level the top.

4 Bake for 20 minutes, then lower the oven temperature to 160°C/325°F/Gas 3 and bake for 1–1¼ hours more, until firm. Cool for 10 minutes in the tin, then turn out on a wire rack to cool.

Banana & Orange Teabread

INGREDIENTS

75g / 3oz / ¾ cup wholemeal flour
75g / 3oz / ¾ cup plain flour
5ml / 1 tsp baking powder
5ml / 1 tsp mixed spice
45ml / 3 tbsp flaked hazelnuts, toasted
2 large ripe bananas
1 egg
30ml / 2 tbsp sunflower oil
30ml / 2 tbsp clear honey
finely grated rind and juice of 1 small orange
DECORATION
4 orange slices, halved
10ml / 2 tsp icing sugar

MAKES 1 LOAF

I Preheat the oven to 180°C/350°F/ Gas 4. Line the base of a 23 x 13cm/9 x 5in loaf tin with grease-proof paper. Grease the paper with a small amount of oil. Sift together the flours, baking powder and mixed spice into a mixing bowl, adding any bran that remains in the sieve. Stir in the hazelnuts. Mix until all ingredients are thoroughly combined.

2 Mash both of the bananas in a mixing bowl with a fork. Beat in the egg, sunflower oil, honey, orange rind and juice. Add to the dry ingredients and mix well.

Spoon the banana mixture into the prepared loaf tin and smooth down the top with a knife or with the back of a spoon.

3 Bake for 40–45 minutes, or until firm and golden brown. Turn out on to a wire rack. Leave to cool until required. Preheat the grill.

4 Sprinkle the orange slices with the icing sugar. Place them on a rack over a grill pan and grill until golden, taking care not to let them burn. Cool slightly, then arrange the slices on top of the loaf.

COOK'S TIP

If you plan to keep the loaf for more than two to three days, omit the orange slices and brush the warm loaf with honey instead. Sprinkle with flaked hazelnuts, if you like.

38

Banana & Cardamom Bread

INGREDIENTS

350ml/12fl oz/1½ cups milk
good pinch of saffron strands
30ml/2 tbsp clear honey, plus extra
for glazing
2 ripe bananas
45ml/3 tbsp caster sugar
900g/2lb/8 cups strong white flour
5ml/1 tsp salt
25g/1oz/2 tbsp butter
2 x 10g/¼oz sachets easy-blend dried yeast
seeds from 6 cardamom pods
115g/4oz/⅔ cup raisins

MAKES 2 LOAVES

1 Heat the milk in a saucepan to simmering point. Pour a little into a cup and crumble in the saffron strands. Set aside to infuse for 5 minutes. Stir the

honey into the remaining milk, pour into a jug and cool to hand-hot. Using a fork, mash the bananas with the caster sugar.

2 Mix the flour and salt in a bowl. Rub in the butter until the mixture resembles breadcrumbs, then stir in the yeast and cardamom seeds.

3 Make a well in the centre and strain in the saffron milk. Add the honey-flavoured milk, mashed banana mixture and raisins. Mix to a soft dough. Add more hand-hot milk, if necessary.

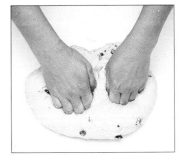

4 Lightly grease two 450g/1lb loaf tins. Knead the dough on a lightly floured surface for 10 minutes. Divide the dough in half and fit each half into a loaf tin.

5 Slip the tins into a lightly oiled plastic bag and leave the loaves to rise for about 1½ hours until they have doubled in bulk. Preheat the oven to 200°C/400°F/Gas 6.

6 Bake the loaves for 20 minutes, then lower the oven temperature to 180°C/350°F/Gas 4 and bake for 20–25 minutes more, or until they sound hollow when rapped underneath. Place on wire racks and brush the tops with honey while the loaves are still warm.

Raisin Bread

INGREDIENTS

175g/6oz/1 cup seedless raisins
75g/3oz/½ cup currants
15ml/1 tbsp brandy
2.5ml/½ tsp grated nutmeg
grated rind of 1 large orange
115g/4oz/½ cup butter
475ml/16fl oz/2 cups milk
675g/1½lb/6 cups plain flour
5ml/1 tsp salt
75g/3oz/6 tbsp caster sugar
15ml/1 tbsp easy-blend dried yeast
1 egg beaten with 15ml/1 tbsp single cream,
for glazing

MAKES 2 LOAVES

1 Mix the dried fruit, brandy, nutmeg and orange rind in a bowl. Melt 50g/2oz/¼ cup of the butter in the milk in a saucepan. Cool to hand-hot.

2 Sift the flour into a large mixing bowl and stir in the salt, sugar and yeast. Add the milk mixture and mix to a dough, then knead on a lightly floured surface for 10 minutes until smooth and elastic.

3 Grease two 450g/1lb loaf tins. Melt the remaining butter. Divide the dough in half. Roll each half to a rectangle measuring 50 x 20cm/20 x 8in.

4 Brush with the melted butter and sprinkle evenly with the raisin mixture. Roll up from a short side, tucking in the ends slightly. Place in the tins, cover and leave in a warm place to rise for about 1½ hours or until doubled in bulk. Preheat the oven to 200°C/400°F/Gas 6.

5 Glaze the loaves with the egg and cream mixture. Bake for 20 minutes, then lower the oven temperature to 180°C/350°F/Gas 4 and bake for 20–25 minutes more, or until golden. Cool on wire racks.

Cranberry & Orange Bread

INGREDIENTS

225g/8oz/2 cups plain flour
10ml/2 tsp baking powder
115g/4oz/½ cup caster sugar
2.5ml/½ tsp salt
grated rind of 1 large orange
175ml/6fl oz/¾ cup orange juice
2 eggs, lightly beaten
75g/3oz/6 tbsp butter, melted
115g/4oz/1 cup fresh cranberries or
bilberries
50g/2oz/½ cup chopped walnuts

MAKES 1 LOAF

1 Preheat the oven to 180°C/350°F/Gas 4. Grease a 450g/1lb loaf tin and base line it with non-stick baking paper.

2 Sift the flour and baking powder into a mixing bowl. Stir in the caster sugar, salt and orange rind. Make a well in the centre and add the orange juice, eggs and melted butter. Stir from the centre until the ingredients are just blended; do not overmix.

3 Add the berries and walnuts and stir gently until just mixed. Spread the mixture in the tin and bake for 45–50 minutes until the loaf is golden and the surface springs back when lightly touched with a finger.

4 Cool the bread in the tin for 10 minutes, then transfer to a wire rack to cool completely. Serve thinly sliced, with butter or cream cheese and jam.

43

Swedish Sultana Bread

INGREDIENTS

175ml/6fl oz/¾ cup milk
150ml/¼ pint/⅔ cup water
15ml/1 tbsp clear honey
225g/8oz/2 cups wholemeal flour
225g/8oz/2 cups strong white flour
5ml/1 tsp salt
10ml/2 tsp easy-blend dried yeast
115g/4oz/⅔ cup sultanas
50g/2oz/½ cup chopped walnuts
milk, for glazing

MAKES 1 LOAF

1 Bring the milk and water to simmering point in a small saucepan. Stir in the honey until dissolved, then pour the milk mixture into a jug and cool to hand-hot.

2 Sift both types of flour into a mixing bowl. Stir in the salt, yeast and sultanas. Set aside 15ml/1 tbsp of the walnuts and add the rest to the bowl. Mix lightly.  Make a well in the centre of the dry ingredients.

3 Add the hand-hot liquid to the well and mix to a soft dough. Add a little extra hand-hot water if necessary. Knead the dough on a lightly floured surface for 10 minutes, making sure that the dried fruit and nuts are well distributed.

4 Lightly grease a baking sheet. Pat the dough into a 28cm/11in long sausage and place it on the baking sheet. Make about four diagonal cuts down the length.

5 Slide the baking sheet into a lightly oiled plastic bag. Leave the bread to rise in a warm place for about 1½ hours. Preheat the oven to 220°C/ 425°F/Gas 7.

6 Brush the dough with milk, sprinkle it with the reserved walnuts and bake for 10 minutes. Lower the oven temperature to 200°C/ 400°F/Gas 6 and 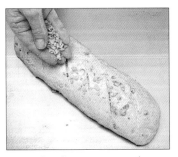 bake for 20 minutes more. Cool on a wire rack.

Plaited Prune Bread

INGREDIENTS

50g/2oz/¼ cup butter
60ml/4 tbsp milk
450g/1lb/4 cups plain flour
2.5ml/½ tsp salt
50g/2oz/¼ cup caster sugar
10g/¼oz sachet easy-blend dried yeast
1 egg, lightly beaten
60ml/4 tbsp hand-hot water
1 egg, beaten with 10ml/2 tsp
water, for glazing
FILLING
200g/7oz/generous 1 cup cooked
stoned prunes
10ml/2 tsp grated lemon rind
5ml/1 tsp grated orange rind
1.5ml/¼ tsp grated nutmeg
40g/1½oz/3 tbsp butter, melted
50g/2oz/½ cup walnuts, very finely chopped
30ml/2 tbsp caster sugar

MAKES 1 LOAF

1 Melt the butter in the milk in a saucepan. Pour into a small jug and cool to hand-hot. Sift the flour into a large mixing bowl and stir in the salt, caster sugar and yeast.

2 Make a well in the centre of the dry ingredients and add the milk mixture, with the beaten egg. Mix in enough of the hand-hot water to make a soft dough. Knead on a lightly floured surface for about 10 minutes, until the dough is smooth and elastic. Return the dough to the clean bowl, cover with a dish cloth and leave in a warm place to rise for about 1½ hours or until doubled in bulk.

3 Lightly grease a large baking sheet. Make the filling by mixing all the ingredients in a bowl. When the dough is ready, punch it down, then roll it out on a lightly floured surface to a rectangle measuring 38 x 25cm/15 x 10in. Transfer to the baking sheet.

4 Spread the filling in the centre of the dough. Cut strips at an angle on either side of the filling, fold up one end neatly, then bring alternate strips up over  the filling to make the plait. Tuck the excess dough underneath at the ends, to neaten.

5 Cover the plait loosely and leave in a warm place to rise again. Preheat the oven to 190°C/375°F/ Gas 5. Glaze the plait with the egg wash and bake for 30 minutes or until golden. Cool on a wire rack.

Apricot Nut Loaf

INGREDIENTS

115g/4oz/⅔ cup dried apricots
1 large orange
75g/3oz/½ cup raisins
150g/5oz/⅔ cup caster sugar
90ml/6 tbsp sunflower oil
2 eggs, lightly beaten
250g/9oz/2¼ cups plain flour
10ml/2 tsp baking powder
2.5ml/½ tsp salt
5ml/1 tsp bicarbonate of soda
50g/2oz/½ cup chopped walnuts
butter, to serve

MAKES 1 LOAF

1 Line a 23 x 13cm/9 x 5in loaf tin with grease-proof paper. Grease the paper. Place the apricots in a bowl, cover with warm water and leave to stand for about 30 minutes.

2 Preheat the oven to 180°C/350°F/Gas 4. Pare the orange thinly and cut the rind into thin matchsticks. Squeeze the pared orange and add water, if necessary, to make 175ml/6fl oz/¾ cup.

3 Drain the apricots and cut into small pieces. Mix the orange rind, apricots and raisins in a bowl and pour over the orange juice. Mix together well. Stir in the sugar, oil and eggs.

4 In a separate bowl, sift together the flour, baking powder, salt and the bicarbonate of soda. Fold into the apricot mixture in three batches. Stir in the walnuts.

5 Spoon the mixture into the prepared tin and bake for 55–60 minutes or until a skewer inserted in the loaf comes out clean. Leave the loaf to cool in the tin for 10 minutes, then transfer to a rack and leave to cool completely. Serve with butter.

Date & Pecan Loaf

Ingredients

175g/6oz/1 cup stoned dates, chopped
175ml/6fl oz/¾ cup boiling water
175g/6oz/1½ cups plain flour
10ml/2 tsp baking powder
2.5ml/½ tsp salt
1.5ml/¼ tsp grated nutmeg
50g/2oz/¼ cup butter, at room temperature
50g/2oz/⅓ cup soft dark brown sugar
50g/2oz/¼ cup caster sugar
1 egg, lightly beaten
30ml/2 tbsp brandy
75g/3oz/¾ cup chopped pecan nuts

Makes 1 loaf

2 Sift the flour, baking powder and salt together. Add the nutmeg. Cream the butter with the sugars in a mixing bowl until light and fluffy. Beat in the egg and brandy.

3 Fold the dry ingredients into the creamed mixture in three batches, alternating with the dates (and soaking water).

4 Fold the chopped pecans into the mixture, scrape it into the tin and level the surface. Bake for 45–50 minutes or until a skewer inserted in the loaf comes out clean. Cool in the tin for 10 minutes before transferring to a wire rack to cool completely.

1 Place the dates in a heatproof bowl and pour over the boiling water. Set aside to cool. Meanwhile preheat the oven to 180°C/350°F/Gas 4. Then grease a

450g/1lb loaf tin and base line with non-stick baking paper.

Malt Loaf

INGREDIENTS

150ml / ¼ pint / ⅔ cup milk
45ml / 3 tbsp malt extract
350g / 12oz / 3 cups plain flour
2.5ml / ½ tsp salt
10g / ¼oz sachet easy-blend dried yeast
30ml / 2 tbsp light muscovado sugar
175g / 6oz / 1 cup sultanas
15ml / 1 tbsp sunflower oil
GLAZE
30ml / 2 tbsp caster sugar
30ml / 2 tbsp water

MAKES 1 LOAF

1 Grease a 450g/1lb loaf tin. Heat the milk in a saucepan to simmering point. Stir in the malt extract until dissolved. Set aside to cool to hand-hot.

2 Mix the flour, salt, yeast and sugar in a bowl. Stir in the sultanas. Make a well in the centre and add the milk mixture and oil. Mix to a soft dough, adding more hand-hot milk if necessary.

3 Knead the dough on a lightly floured surface for 10 minutes, until smooth and elastic. Fit it in the loaf tin, cover and leave in a warm place to rise for about 1½ hours until it has doubled in bulk. Preheat the oven to 190°C/375°F/Gas 5.

4 Bake the loaf for 30 minutes, until it sounds hollow when rapped underneath. Meanwhile make the glaze. Dissolve the caster sugar in the water in a small pan. Bring to the boil, stirring, then lower the heat and simmer for 1 minute.

5 Put the loaf on a wire rack and brush it with the glaze while still hot. Leave the loaf to cool. Serve with butter and a fruit jam, if liked.

VARIATION

Make malt buns by dividing the loaf into 10 pieces, shaping them into rounds and leaving them to rise. Bake the buns for 15 minutes, then glaze.

Dried Cherry Muffins

1 In a mixing bowl, combine the yogurt and cherries. Cover and leave to stand for 30 minutes.

2 Preheat the oven to 180°C/350°F/Gas 4. Grease a 16-cup bun tin or arrange 16 double paper cake cases on baking sheets.

3 With an electric mixer, cream the butter and sugar together until light and fluffy.

4 Add the eggs, one at a time, beating well after each addition. Add the vanilla essence and the cherry mixture and stir to blend. Set aside.

5 In another bowl, sift together the flour, baking powder, bicarbonate of soda and salt. Fold into the cherry mixture in three batches.

6 Fill the prepared cups two-thirds full. Bake for about 20 minutes, until the tops spring back when touched lightly. Transfer to a wire rack to cool.

52

INGREDIENTS

250ml/8fl oz/1 cup natural yogurt
175g/6oz/1 cup dried cherries
115g/4oz/½ cup butter, at room temperature
175g/6oz/¾ cup caster sugar
2 eggs
5ml/1 tsp vanilla essence
200g/7oz/1¾ cups plain flour
10ml/2 tsp baking powder
5ml/1 tsp bicarbonate of soda
pinch of salt

MAKES 16

Chocolate Chip Muffins

INGREDIENTS

115g/4oz/½ cup unsalted butter
or margarine
65g/2½oz/generous ¼ cup caster sugar
30ml/2 tbsp soft dark brown sugar
2 eggs, beaten
175g/6oz/1½ cups plain flour
5ml/1 tsp baking powder
120ml/4fl oz/½ cup milk
175g/6oz/1 cup chocolate chips

MAKES 10

3 Divide half the mixture between 10 muffin cups or cases and sprinkle the chocolate chips over, then cover with the remaining mixture. Bake for 20–25 minutes, or

until the muffins are well risen. The tops of the muffins should spring back when lightly touched. If paper cases were not used, cool in the cups for 5 minutes before turning out. Serve warm or cool.

53

1 Preheat the oven to 190°C/375°F/ Gas 5. Lightly grease a 12-cup muffin tin, or use paper cases. Using an electric mixer, cream together the unsalted butter or margarine with the caster and soft dark brown sugar until light and fluffy. Beat in the eggs, a little at a time, adding a small amount of flour if the mixture shows signs of curdling.

2 Sift the flour and baking powder into a separate bowl. Fold into the creamed mixture in stages, alternately with the milk.

Apple & Cranberry Muffins

INGREDIENTS

150g / 5oz / 1¼ cups plain flour
5ml / 1 tsp baking powder
2.5ml / ½ tsp bicarbonate of soda
5ml / 1 tsp ground cinnamon
2.5ml / ½ tsp grated nutmeg
2.5ml / ½ tsp ground allspice
1.5ml / ¼ tsp ground ginger
1.5ml / ¼ tsp salt
50g / 2oz / ¼ cup unsalted butter or margarine
1 egg, beaten
90ml / 6 tbsp caster sugar
grated rind of 1 large orange
*120ml / 4fl oz / ½ cup freshly squeezed
orange juice*
1-2 eating apples
115g / 4oz / 1 cup cranberries
50g / 2oz / ½ cup chopped walnuts
icing sugar, for dusting

MAKES 12

1 Preheat the oven to 180°C/350°F/Gas 4. Lightly grease a 12-cup muffin tin. Sift the flour, baking powder, bicarbonate of soda, spices and salt into a large bowl. Melt the butter or margarine.

2 Whisk together the beaten egg and melted butter or margarine. Add the sugar, orange rind and juice, and mix together well.

3 Peel, quarter, and core the apples, then chop coarsely. Make a well in the centre of the dry ingredients and pour in the egg mixture. With a large metal spoon, stir for just long enough to moisten the flour – the mixture need not be smooth.

4 Fold the apples, cranberries and walnuts into the mixture. Spoon the mixture into the muffin cups, filling them three-quarters full. Bake for 25–30 minutes until the muffins are well risen. The tops should spring back when lightly touched. Cool in the cups for 5 minutes before turning out. Serve warm or cool, dusted with icing sugar.

54

Chocolate Nut Cookies

INGREDIENTS

25g/1oz plain chocolate, broken into squares
25g/1oz bitter cooking chocolate,
broken into squares
225g/8oz/2 cups plain flour
2.5ml/½ tsp salt
225g/8oz/1 cup unsalted butter,
at room temperature
225g/8oz/1 cup caster sugar
2 eggs, beaten
5ml/1 tsp vanilla essence
115g/4oz/1 cup walnuts, finely chopped

MAKES 50

1 Combine the plain and bitter chocolate squares in a heatproof bowl. Bring a small saucepan of water to the boil, remove from the heat and place the bowl on top. Set aside until the chocolate has completely melted, then stir until smooth. Sift the flour and salt into a small bowl; set aside.

2 Using an electric mixer, cream the butter in a mixing bowl until soft. Add the sugar and beat until light and fluffy. Beat in the eggs and vanilla essence, a little at a time, then stir in the melted chocolate. Add the flour mixture and the nuts and fold in gently until well mixed together.

3 Divide the mixture equally into four parts, and, with your hands, roll each into a log, about 5cm/2in in diameter. Wrap each chocolate log tightly in foil and chill overnight in the fridge, or place the logs in the freezer for several hours until firm.

4 Preheat the oven to 190°C/375°F/Gas 5. Grease two or three baking sheets. With a sharp knife, cut the logs into 5mm/¼in slices. Place the rounds on the baking sheets and bake for 10 minutes or until lightly coloured. Cool on wire racks.

Chocolate-tipped Hazelnut Crescents

INGREDIENTS

225g / 8oz / 2 cups plain flour
pinch of salt
225g / 8oz / 1 cup unsalted butter, softened
50g / 2oz / 1/4 cup caster sugar
15ml / 1 tbsp hazelnut liqueur or water
5ml / 1 tsp vanilla essence
425g / 15oz milk chocolate
50g / 2oz / 1/2 cup roasted chopped hazelnuts
icing sugar, for dusting

MAKES ABOUT 35

1 Preheat the oven to 160°C/325°F/Gas 3. Grease two large baking sheets. Sift the flour and salt together into a bowl and set aside.

2 Using an electric mixer, cream the butter in a mixing bowl. Add the sugar and beat until fluffy, then beat in the hazelnut liqueur or water and vanilla essence. Gently stir in the flour mixture, until just blended. Set aside 350g/12oz of the chocolate and grate the rest into the mixture. Add the chopped hazelnuts and fold in lightly.

3 With very light-ly floured hands, shape the dough into about 35 5 x 1cm/2 x 1/2in crescents. Place on the baking sheets, 5cm/2in apart. Bake for about  20–25 minutes until golden. Cool on the baking sheets for 10 minutes, then use a palette knife to transfer to wire racks to cool completely.

4 Line the clean baking sheets with non-stick baking paper. Dust the crescents with icing sugar. Melt the remaining chocolate in a bowl over hot water. Using tongs, dip half of each crescent into the chocolate, place on the prepared baking sheets and chill until the chocolate has set.

Apricot Yogurt Cookies

INGREDIENTS

175g/6oz/1½ cups plain flour
5ml/1 tsp baking powder
5ml/1 tsp ground cinnamon
75g/3oz/1 cup rolled oats
75g/3oz/½ cup soft light brown sugar
115g/4oz/⅔ cup ready-to-eat dried apricots
15ml/1 tbsp flaked hazelnuts or almonds
150ml/¼ pint/⅔ cup natural yogurt, plus
extra yogurt or milk (see method)
45ml/3 tbsp sunflower oil
demerara sugar, to sprinkle

MAKES 16

1 Preheat the oven to 190°C/375°F/ Gas 5. Lightly grease a large baking sheet with oil. Sift together the plain flour, baking powder and cinnamon into a large mixing bowl. Using a wooden spoon stir in the oats, light brown sugar, dried apricots and nuts.

2 In a small bowl, whisk the yogurt and oil together. Pour into the flour mixture and mix to a firm dough. If necessary, add a little extra yogurt or milk.

3 With floured hands, form the mixture into 16 rough mounds. Place them on the baking sheet, leaving room for spreading, then flatten with a fork.

Sprinkle with sugar and bake for 15–20 minutes. Cool for 5 minutes, then transfer to a wire rack.

COOK'S TIP

These cookies do not keep very well, so it is best to eat them within 2 days, or freeze them. Open freeze, pack in polythene bags, label and freeze for up to 4 months.

Florentines

INGREDIENTS

40g / 1 ½oz / 3 tbsp unsalted butter
120ml / 4fl oz / ½ cup whipping cream
115g / 4oz / ½ cup caster sugar
115g / 4oz / 1 cup flaked almonds
50g / 2oz / ⅓ cup chopped mixed peel
40g / 1 ½oz / ¼ cup glacé cherries, chopped
65g / 2½oz / generous ½ cup plain flour, sifted
225g / 8oz plain chocolate, broken into squares
5ml / 1 tsp sunflower oil

MAKES ABOUT 36

1 Preheat the oven to 180°C/350°F/Gas 4. Grease two baking sheets. Melt the butter, cream and sugar in a saucepan, then bring to the boil. Remove from the heat and mix in the almonds, peel, cherries and flour.

2 Drop small spoonfuls of the mixture 5cm/2in apart on the prepared baking sheets. Flatten with a fork. Bake for 10 minutes or until the florentines start to colour at the edges. Remove from the oven and quickly neaten the edges with a knife or round biscuit cutter. Use a metal palette knife to transfer the florentines to a clean, flat surface.

3 Melt the chocolate in a bowl over hot water. Add the oil and stir until well blended. Use the palette knife to spread the smooth underside of the cooked florentines with a thin coating of melted chocolate. Arrange on a rack and leave until almost set.

4 Draw a serrated knife across the surface of the chocolate, using a very slight sawing action, to make wavy lines. Allow to set completely before serving.

COOK'S TIP
When tidying the edges on the freshly cooked florentines, try to work fast, or they will harden on the baking sheets. If necessary, return them to the oven for a few minutes to soften.

60

Pecan Bars

INGREDIENTS

225g/8oz/2 cups plain flour
pinch of salt
115g/4oz/½ cup caster sugar
115g/4oz/½ cup unsalted butter
or margarine
1 egg
finely grated rind of 1 lemon
TOPPING
175g/6oz/¾ cup unsalted butter
60ml/4 tbsp clear honey
50g/2oz/¼ cup sugar
150g/5oz/scant 1 cup soft dark brown sugar
75ml/5 tbsp whipping cream
450g/1lb/4 cups pecan nuts, halved

MAKES 36

1 Preheat the oven to 190°C/375°F/Gas 5. Lightly grease a 41 x 26cm/15½ x 10½in Swiss roll tin. Sift the flour and salt into a mixing bowl. Stir in the sugar. Add the butter or margarine and cut in with a knife, then rub in until the mixture resembles coarse breadcrumbs.

2 Add the egg and lemon rind and mix with a fork until the mixture just holds together. Spoon the mixture into the prepared tin, then press it out evenly.  Prick all over with a fork and leave to chill in the fridge for about 10 minutes.

3 Bake the dough base for 15 minutes, then remove from the oven while you make the topping. Keep the oven on. Melt the butter, honey and both sugars in a  saucepan. Bring to the boil and boil without stirring for 2 minutes. Remove from the heat and stir in the cream and pecan nuts. Pour the mixture over the dough base, return the tin to the oven and bake for 25 minutes more. Cool in the tin.

4 Run a knife around the edge of the dough. Invert on to a clean baking sheet, then place another sheet on top and invert again. Dip a sharp knife into very hot water and cut into squares for serving.

Savoury Pies

What could be nicer than a melt in the mouth savoury pie. From the traditional Steak, Kidney & Mushroom to the succulent Salmon and Ginger with Lemon Thyme & Lime, there's sure to be a pie to suit every occasion.

Old-fashioned Chicken Pie

INGREDIENTS

1 chicken, about 1.75kg/4-4½lb
1 onion, quartered
1 tarragon or rosemary sprig
300ml/½ pint/1¼ cups water
25g/1oz/2 tbsp butter
115g/4oz/1 cup small button mushrooms
30ml/2 tbsp plain flour
115g/4oz cooked ham, diced
30ml/2 tbsp chopped fresh parsley
450g/1lb fresh or thawed frozen puff pastry
1 egg, beaten
salt and ground black pepper

SERVES 4

1 Preheat the oven to 200°C/400°F/Gas 6. Put the chicken in a casserole, with the onion, herb sprig and water. Cover with a lid and bake for about 1¼ hours or until tender.

2 Transfer the chicken to a plate and remove the skin. Strain the cooking liquid into a measuring jug or bowl. Set aside to cool. Remove the meat from the chicken bones, cutting it into large chunks.

3 Melt the butter in a saucepan. Cook the mushrooms for 2–3 minutes. Meanwhile skim off any fat from the surface of the chicken stock; add water to make the stock up to 300ml/½ pint/1¼ cups.

4 Sprinkle flour over the button mushrooms, then gradually stir in the chicken stock. Bring to the boil, stirring, then add the ham, chicken and parsley, with salt and pepper to taste. Turn into one large or four individual pie dishes and leave to cool.

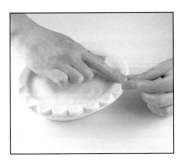

5 Roll out the pastry on a lightly floured surface to a round or oval 5cm/2in larger than the pie dish. Cut a narrow strip to place around the edge of the dish, brush it lightly with beaten egg, then fit the lid in place. Scallop the edges and knock up the sides with the back of a knife. Cut a hole in the centre of the pie(s) to allow steam to escape. Decorate with pastry leaves.

6 Heat the oven to 200°C/400°F/Gas 6 again. Glaze the pastry with beaten egg. Bake until well risen and golden brown. Individual pies will require 25–35 minutes; a large pie 35–45 minutes.

66

Pennsylvania Dutch Ham & Apple Pie

INGREDIENTS

5 cooking apples
60ml/4 tbsp soft light brown sugar
15ml/1 tbsp plain flour
4ml/¾ tsp ground cloves
4ml/¾ tsp ground black pepper
175g/6oz sliced baked ham
25g/1oz/2 tbsp butter or margarine
60ml/4 tbsp whipping cream
1 egg yolk
PASTRY
225g/8oz/2 cups plain flour
2.5ml/½ tsp salt
75g/3oz/6 tbsp cold butter, cut in pieces
50g/2oz/4 tbsp cold margarine, cut in pieces
50-120ml/2-4fl oz/¼-½ cup iced water

SERVES 6–8

1 To make the crust, sift the flour and salt into a bowl. Rub in the butter and margarine until the mixture resembles coarse crumbs. Stir in enough water to bind, gather the dough into two balls, and wrap in clear film. Chill for 20 minutes. Preheat the oven to 220°C/425°F/Gas 7.

2 Quarter, core, peel, and thinly slice the apples. Place in a bowl and toss with the sugar, flour, cloves and pepper, to coat evenly. Set aside.

3 Roll out one dough ball 3mm/⅛in thick. Fit in a 25cm/10in pie dish. Leave an overhang.

4 Arrange half the ham slices in the bottom. Top with a layer of apple slices. Dot with half the butter or margarine. Repeat layering, finishing with apples. Dot with butter or margarine. Pour over 45ml/3 tbsp of the whipping cream, in an even layer.

5 Roll out the remaining dough and put on top of the pie. Fold the top edge under the bottom crust and press to seal. Roll out the dough scraps and stamp out decorative shapes. Arrange on top of the pie. Crimp the edge using your finger and a fork. Cut steam vents at regular intervals. Mix the egg yolk and remaining cream and brush on top of the pie to glaze. Avoid clogging the steam vents.

6 Bake for about 10 minutes. Reduce the heat to 180°C/350°F/Gas 4. Bake for 30–35 minutes more, until golden. Serve hot.

Bacon & Egg Pie

INGREDIENTS

*450-500g / 1-1¼lb shortcrust pastry, thawed
if frozen
30ml / 2 tbsp oil
4 rindless smoked bacon rashers, cut in
4cm / 1½in pieces
1 small onion, finely chopped
5 eggs
25ml / 1½ tbsp chopped fresh parsley (optional)
salt and ground black pepper
beaten egg or milk, to glaze*

SERVES 4

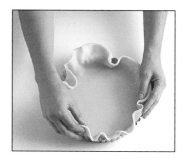

1 Use two-thirds of the pastry to line a 20cm/8in flan ring. Chill for 20 minutes. Pre-heat the oven to 200°C/400°F/Gas 6. Heat the oil in a pan and fry the bacon and onion until the onion is soft, and the bacon is starting to crisp. Drain on kitchen paper.

2 Cover the bottom of the pastry case with the bacon mixture, spreading it evenly, then break the eggs on to the bacon, spacing them evenly apart. Carefully tilt the flan tin so the egg whites flow together. Sprinkle the eggs with the chopped fresh parsley, if using, plenty of black pepper, and just a little salt if the bacon is very salty. Place a baking sheet in the oven to heat.

3 Roll out the remaining pastry, dampen the edges and place over the filling. Press to seal the edges, then remove excess pastry and use for pastry leaves. Decorate the pie, brush it with egg or milk and make a hole in the centre.

4 Place the pie on the baking sheet and bake for 10 minutes, then reduce the oven temperature to 180°C/350°F/Gas 4 and bake for 20 minutes. Leave to cool before cutting.

70

Greek Lamb Pie

INGREDIENTS

sunflower oil, for brushing
450g / 1lb lean minced lamb
1 medium onion, sliced
1 garlic clove, crushed
400g / 14oz can plum tomatoes
30ml / 2 tbsp chopped fresh mint
5ml / 1 tsp grated nutmeg
350g / 12oz young spinach leaves
275g / 10oz packet filo pastry
5ml / 1 tsp sesame seeds
salt and ground black pepper

SERVES 4

4 Lightly brush each sheet of filo pastry with oil and lay in overlapping layers in the tin, leaving enough overhanging to wrap over the top.

5 Spoon in the meat and spinach. Wrap the pastry over to enclose the filling; scrunch it slightly. Sprinkle with sesame seeds and bake the lamb filo pie for about  25–30 minutes, or until golden and crisp. Serve the pie hot, using a sharp knife to cut through the filo.

1 Preheat the oven to 200°C/400°F/Gas 6. Lightly oil a 23cm/9in round springform tin.

2 Fry the mince and onion without fat in a non-stick pan until golden. Add the garlic, tomatoes, mint, nutmeg, salt and pepper. Bring to the boil, stirring. Simmer, stirring occasionally, until most of the liquid has evaporated.

3 Wash the spinach and remove any tough stalks. Place the wet leaves in a saucepan, cover and cook for about 2 minutes, until wilted.

Lamb Pie with Pear, Ginger & Mint Sauce

INGREDIENTS

1 boned mid-loin of lamb, about 1kg/2¼lb
after boning
15ml/1 tbsp oil
25g/1oz/2 tbsp butter, plus extra for greasing
8 large sheets filo pastry
salt and ground black pepper
flat leaf parsley, to garnish
STUFFING & SAUCE
1 small onion, chopped
15g/½oz/1 tbsp butter
115g/4oz/1 cup wholemeal breadcrumbs
grated rind of 1 lemon
1.5ml/¼ tsp ground ginger
400g/14oz can pears
1 egg, beaten
10ml/2 tsp finely chopped fresh mint, plus
a small sprig, to garnish

SERVES 6

1 Make the stuffing. Fry the onion in the butter until soft. Tip into a bowl and add the breadcrumbs, lemon rind and ginger. Drain the pears, reserving the juice and half the fruit. Chop the remaining pears and add them to the mixture; season and bind with the egg. Spread the loin out flat, fat-side down, and season. Place the stuffing along the middle of the loin and roll up carefully.

2 Holding the meat firmly, close the opening with a trussing needle threaded with string. Heat the oil in heavy frying pan and brown the roll slowly on all sides, until well coloured. Leave to cool, and store in the fridge until needed.

3 Preheat the oven to 200°C/400°F/Gas 6. Melt the butter. Keeping the remainder of the filo covered, brush two sheets with a little butter. Overlap by about 13cm/5in to make a square. Place the next two sheets on top and brush with butter. Continue until the filo has all been used.

4 Remove the string from the lamb and place the roll diagonally across one corner of the pastry, so that it sits within the pastry square, without overhanging the edges. Fold the corner of the pastry over the lamb, fold in the sides, and brush with melted butter. Roll up neatly. Place the roll join-side down on a greased baking sheet and bake for 40 minutes, covering it with foil if it browns too rapidly and looks as if it might burn.

5 Meanwhile, make the sauce. Purée the reserved pears, juice and mint. Pour into a sauce-boat and garnish with a mint sprig. Place the lamb on a platter, garnish with flat leaf parsley and serve with the pear, ginger and mint sauce.

Mixed Game Pie

INGREDIENTS

*450g/1lb game meat, off the bone, diced
(plus the carcasses and bones)
1 small onion, halved
2 bay leaves
2 carrots, halved
a few black peppercorns
15ml/1 tbsp oil
75g/3oz/½ cup rindless streaky
bacon, chopped
15ml/1 tbsp plain flour
45ml/3 tbsp sweet sherry or Madeira
10ml/2 tsp ground ginger
grated rind and juice of ½ orange
350g/12oz puff pastry, thawed if frozen
salt and ground black pepper
beaten egg or milk, to glaze
redcurrant or sage and apple jelly, to serve*

SERVES 4

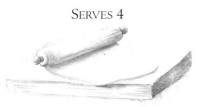

1 Place the carcasses and bones in a pan, with any giblets and half the onion, the bay leaves, carrots and peppercorns. Cover with water and bring to the boil. Simmer until reduced to about 300ml/ ½ pint/1¼ cups, then strain the stock into a jug.

2 Chop the other onion half and fry in the oil until soft. Add the bacon and meat and fry quickly to seal. Sprinkle on the flour and stir until beginning to brown. Gradually add the stock, stirring constantly as it thickens, then add the sherry or Madeira, ground ginger, orange rind and juice, and salt and pepper. Simmer for 20 minutes, until thick and flavoursome. Check the seasoning.

3 Transfer to a 900ml/1½ pint/3¾ cup pie dish and allow to cool slightly. Put a pie funnel in the centre of the filling to help hold up the pastry.

4 Preheat the oven to 220°C/425°F/Gas 7. Roll out the pastry to 2.5cm/1in larger than the dish. Cut off a 1cm/½in strip all round. Damp the rim of the dish and press on the strip of pastry. Damp the pastry strip, then lift the pastry carefully over the pie, sealing the edges at the rim. Trim off the excess pastry and scallop the edge. Decorate the top, then brush the pie with egg or milk to glaze.

5 Bake for 15 minutes, then reduce the heat to 190°C/375°F/Gas 5, for 25–30 minutes more. Serve with redcurrant or sage and apple jelly.

Steak, Kidney & Mushroom Pie

INGREDIENTS

30ml/2 tbsp oil
1 onion, chopped
115g/4oz rindless streaky bacon, chopped
500g/1¼lb chuck steak, diced
30ml/2 tbsp plain flour
115g/4oz lamb's kidneys
large bouquet garni
400ml/14fl oz/1¾ cups beef stock
175g/6oz/1½ cups button mushrooms
225g/8oz puff pastry, thawed if frozen
salt and ground black pepper
beaten egg, to glaze

SERVES 4

1 Preheat the oven to 160°C/325°F/Gas 3. Heat the oil in a heavy-based pan, then cook the onion and bacon until lightly browned.

2 Toss the steak in the flour. Stir the meat into the pan in batches and cook, stirring, until browned.

3 Toss the kidneys in flour and add to the pan with the bouquet garni. Pour in the stock, transfer to a casserole, fit the lid and cook in the oven for 2 hours. Stir in the mushrooms and seasoning and set the casserole aside to cool completely.

4 Preheat the oven to 220°C/425°F/Gas 7. Roll out the pastry to 2cm/¾in larger than the top of a 1.2 litre/2 pint/5 cup pie dish. Cut off a narrow strip from the pastry and fit around the dampened rim of the dish. Brush the pastry strip with water.

5 Tip the meat mixture into the dish. Lay the pastry over the dish, press the edges to seal, then crimp them and knock them up with the back of a knife. Make a small slit in the pastry, brush with beaten egg and bake for 20 minutes. Lower the oven temperature to 180°C/350°F/Gas 4 and bake for 20 minutes more, until the pastry is golden.

Golden Fish Pie

INGREDIENTS

675g / 1½lb white fish fillets
300ml / ½ pint / 1¼ cups milk
black peppercorns, bay leaf and onion slices,
to flavour
115g / 4oz cooked, peeled prawns, thawed
if frozen
115g / 4oz / ½ cup butter
50g / 2oz / ½ cup plain flour
300ml / ½ pint / 1¼ cups single cream
75g / 3oz / ¾ cup grated Gruyère cheese
1 bunch watercress, leaves only, chopped
5ml / 1 tsp Dijon mustard
5 sheets filo pastry
salt and ground black pepper

SERVES 4–6

1 Place the fish fillets in a pan, pour over the milk and add the flavouring ingredients. Bring just to the boil, then cover and simmer for about 10–12 minutes, until the fish is just cooked through. Watch the pan closely, as milk readily boils over.

2 Lift out the fish, remove the skin and bones, then roughly flake it into a shallow ovenproof dish. Scatter the prawns over. Strain the milk and reserve.

3 Melt 50g/2oz/4 tbsp of the butter in a pan. Stir in the flour and cook for 1 minute. Stir in the reserved milk and cream. Bring to the boil, stirring, then simmer for 2–3 minutes, still stirring, until the sauce has thickened and is rich and creamy.

4 Remove the pan from the heat and stir in the Gruyère, watercress, mustard and seasoning to taste. Pour over the fish and leave to cool.

5 Preheat the oven to 190°C/375°F/ Gas 5. Melt the rest of the butter. Brush one sheet of filo pastry with butter. Crumple it loosely and place on top of the filling. Repeat with the rest of the filo sheets and butter, until they are all used up and the pie is completely covered.

6 Bake in the oven for 25–30 minutes, until the filo pastry is golden and crisp, and the filling is piping hot. Serve the pie at once. Use a large, very sharp knife to cut the pie.

Salmon & Ginger Pie, with Lemon Thyme & Lime

INGREDIENTS

800g/1¾lb middle cut of salmon
45ml/3 tbsp walnut oil
15ml/1 tbsp fresh lime juice
10ml/2 tsp chopped fresh lemon thyme,
plus extra sprigs to garnish
30ml/2 tbsp white wine
400g/14oz puff pastry, thawed if frozen
50g/2oz/½ cup flaked almonds
3-4 pieces of drained stem ginger in
syrup, chopped
salt and ground black pepper
beaten egg, to glaze

SERVES 4–6

1 Split the salmon in half, remove the bones and skin, and divide into four fillets. Mix the oil, lime juice, thyme, wine and pepper to taste, and pour over the fish in a shallow dish. Cover closely and leave the salmon to marinate overnight in the fridge.

2 Divide the pastry into two pieces, one slightly larger than the other, and roll out – the smaller piece should be large enough to take two of the salmon fillets side by side and the second piece about 5cm/2in larger all round. Drain the fillets and discard the marinade.

3 Preheat the oven to 190°C/350°F/ Gas 5. Place the smaller piece of pastry on a baking sheet, then arrange two of the fillets on top. Season. Sprinkle the fish with the almonds, ginger and a little more lemon thyme, if you like. Cover these fillets with the other two salmon fillets.

4 Season again, cover with the second piece of pastry, tuck the edges under the pastry base and seal well. Brush with beaten egg and decorate with any leftover pastry. Bake for 40 minutes until the crust is golden. Serve on a bed of lemon thyme.

80

Chestnut & Vegetable Pie

INGREDIENTS

450g/1lb puff pastry, thawed if frozen
450g/1lb Brussels sprouts, trimmed
45ml/3 tbsp sunflower oil
1 large red pepper, sliced
1 large onion, sliced
about 16 canned chestnuts, peeled if fresh
1 egg yolk, beaten with 15ml/1 tbsp water
SAUCE
40g/1½oz/scant ½ cup plain flour
40g/1½oz/3 tbsp butter
300ml/½ pint/1¼ cups milk
75g/3oz/¾ cup grated Cheddar cheese
30ml/2 tbsp dry sherry
good pinch of dried sage
45ml/3 tbsp chopped fresh parsley
salt and ground black pepper

SERVES 6

1 Roll out the pastry to make two large rectangles, roughly the size of a large pie dish. The pastry should be about 5mm/¼in thick and one rectangle should be slightly larger than the other. Set the pastry aside in the fridge to rest.

2 Blanch the Brussels sprouts for 4 minutes in 300ml/½ pint/1¼ cups boiling water, then drain, reserving the water. Refresh the sprouts under cold running water, drain and set aside.

3 Heat the oil in a frying pan and lightly fry the red pepper and onion for 5 minutes. Set the pan aside until later. Cut each chestnut in half.

4 Make the sauce by beating all the flour, butter and milk together over a medium heat. Beat the sauce continuously as it comes to the boil, then stir until it is thickened and smooth. Stir in the reserved sprout water and the cheese, sherry, sage and seasoning. Simmer for 3 minutes to reduce, then mix in the chopped fresh parsley.

5 Fit the larger piece of pastry into your pie dish and layer the sprouts, chestnuts, pepper and onions on top. Trickle the sauce over the top, making sure it  seeps through to moisten the vegetables. Brush the pastry edges with the beaten egg yolk and water and fit the second pastry sheet on top, pressing the edges well to seal them securely.

6 Trim, crimp and knock up the edges, then slash the centre several times. Glaze with the egg yolk. Set aside to rest somewhere cool while you preheat the oven to 200°C/400°F/Gas 6. Bake for about 30–40 minutes, until golden brown and crisp.

Green Lentil Filo Pie

INGREDIENTS

175g/6oz/1 cup green lentils, soaked for
30 minutes in water to cover, drained
2 bay leaves
2 onions, sliced
1.2 litres/2 pints/5 cups stock
175g/6oz/¾ cup butter, melted
225g/8oz/1¼ cups long grain rice,
ideally basmati
60ml/4 tbsp chopped fresh parsley, plus a few
sprigs to garnish
30ml/2 tbsp chopped fresh dill
1 egg, beaten
225g/8oz/2 cups mushrooms, sliced
about 8 sheets filo pastry
3 eggs, hard-boiled and sliced
salt and ground black pepper

SERVES 6

1 Cover the lentils with water, then simmer with the bay leaves, one onion and half the stock for 20–25 minutes, or until tender. Season well. Set aside to cool.

2 Gently fry the remaining onion in another saucepan in 25g/1oz/2 tbsp of the butter, for 5 minutes. Stir in the rice and the rest of the stock. Season, bring to the boil, then cover and simmer for 12 minutes for basmati, 15 minutes for long grain. Leave to stand, uncovered, for 5 minutes, then stir in the fresh herbs and the beaten egg.

3 Fry the mushrooms in 45ml/3 tbsp of the butter for 5 minutes, until they are just soft. Set aside to cool. Preheat the oven to 190°C/375°F/Gas 5.

4 Brush the inside of a large, shallow ovenproof dish with more butter. Lay the sheets of filo in it, covering the base but making sure most of the filo hangs over the sides. Brush the sheets of filo well with butter as you go and overlap the pastry as required. Ensure there is a lot of pastry to fold over the mounded green lentil filling.

5 Into the pastry lining, layer rice, lentils and mushrooms, repeating the layers at least once and tucking the sliced egg in between. Season as you layer and form an even mound of filling. Bring up the sheets of pastry over the filling, scrunching the top into attractive folds. Brush all over with the rest of the butter and set aside to chill and firm up.

6 Bake the pie for about 45 minutes, until golden and crisp. Allow it to stand for 10 minutes before serving, garnished with parsley.

84

Curried Parsnip Pie

INGREDIENTS

8 baby onions, peeled
2 carrots, thinly sliced
2 large parsnips, thinly sliced
25g/1oz/2 tbsp butter
30ml/2 tbsp wholemeal flour
15ml/1 tbsp mild curry or tikka paste
300ml/½ pint/1¼ cups milk
115g/4oz/1 cup grated mature
Cheddar cheese
45ml/3 tbsp chopped fresh coriander
salt and ground black pepper
1 egg yolk, beaten with 10ml/2 tsp water
coriander or parsley sprig, to garnish
PASTRY
115g/4oz/½ cup butter
225g/8oz/2 cups plain flour
5ml/1 tsp dried thyme or oregano
cold water, to mix

SERVES 4

1 Preheat the oven to 200°C/ 400°F/ Gas 6. Make the pastry. Rub the butter into the flour until it resembles coarse breadcrumbs. Season well and stir in the thyme or oregano, then mix to a firm dough with cold water. Chill until required.

2 Boil the baby onions, carrots and parsnips in salted water for 5 minutes, then drain, reserving 300ml/ ½ pint/ 1¼ cups of the cooking liquid.

3 Melt the butter, stir in the flour and curry or tikka paste, then gradually whisk in the reserved liquid and milk, until thick and smooth. Stir in the cheese and seasoning, then add the vegetables and the chopped coriander. Pour into a pie dish, fix a pie funnel in the centre and allow to cool.

4 Roll out the pastry to 2cm/¾in larger than the top of the pie dish. Cut off a narrow strip from the pastry, brush with the egg yolk wash and fit around the rim of the dish. Brush again with egg yolk wash. Using a rolling pin, lift the rolled-out pastry over the pie top and fit over the funnel, pressing it down well on to the strips underneath. Trim the over-hanging pastry and crimp the edges. Cut a hole for the funnel, decorate with pastry leaves and brush all over with the remaining egg yolk wash.

5 Bake the pie for 25–30 minutes until golden brown and crisp. Serve, garnished with a coriander or parsley sprig.

Spinach & Feta Pie

INGREDIENTS

900g/2lb fresh spinach, chopped
25g/1oz/2 tbsp butter or margarine
2 onions, chopped
2 garlic cloves, crushed
275g/10oz feta cheese, crumbled
115g/4oz/⅔ cup pine nuts
5 eggs, beaten
2 saffron strands, soaked in 10ml/2 tsp boiling water
5ml/1 tsp paprika
1.5ml/¼ tsp ground cumin
1.5ml/¼ tsp ground cinnamon
14 sheets filo pastry
about 60ml/4 tbsp olive oil
salt and ground black pepper
Cos lettuce leaves, to serve

SERVES 6

1 Place the spinach in a large colander, sprinkle with a little salt, rub it in and leave for 30 minutes to drain the excess liquid.

2 Preheat the oven to 180°C/350°F/Gas 4. Melt the butter or margarine in a large pan and fry the onion until golden. Add the garlic, cheese and pine nuts. Remove from the heat and stir in the eggs, spinach, saffron and spices. Season with salt and pepper and mix well. Set the mixture aside.

3 Grease a large rectangular baking dish. Take seven of the sheets of filo and brush one side with a little olive oil. Place in the dish, overlapping the sheets so that the bottom is covered. Leave plenty of overhang to cover the filling later.

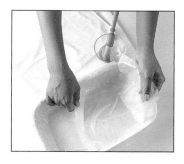

4 Spoon all the spinach mixture into the dish and carefully drizzle 30ml/2 tbsp of the remaining olive oil over the top. Fold the overhanging pastry over the filling. Cut the remaining pastry sheets to the size of the dish and brush each one with more olive oil. Arrange on top of the filling.

5 Brush with water to prevent curling, then bake the pie for about 30 minutes, until the pastry is golden brown. Serve warm or cold, with a salad of crisp Cos lettuce leaves.

COOK'S TIP
Cheddar, Parmesan or any hard cheese can be added to this dish as well as the feta.

88

Sweet Pies

For the perfect end to any meal choose from childhood favourites such as Open Apple Pie or Cherry Lattice Pie. Or, for an unforgettable finale, indulge yourself with the very tempting velvety-smooth richness of the Chocolate Cheesecake Pie.

Plum Pie

INGREDIENTS

275g/10oz/2½ cups plain flour
5ml/1 tsp salt
75g/3oz/⅓ cup chilled unsalted butter
50g/2oz/½ cup chilled vegetable fat or lard
60-120ml/4-8 tbsp iced water
milk, for glazing
FILLING
900g/2lb red or purple plums,
halved and stoned
grated rind of 1 lemon
15ml/1 tbsp lemon juice
115-175g/4-6oz/½-¾ cup caster sugar
45ml/3 tbsp quick-cooking tapioca
pinch of salt
2.5ml/½ tsp ground cinnamon
1.5ml/¼ tsp grated nutmeg

SERVES 8

1 Sift the flour and salt into a bowl. Rub in the butter and vegetable fat or lard until the mixture resembles breadcrumbs. Stir in just enough iced water to bind the pastry. Gather into two balls, one slightly larger than the other. Wrap and chill for 20 minutes.

2 Preheat the oven to 220°C/425°F/Gas 7. Line a baking sheet with greaseproof paper. Set it aside. Roll out the larger piece of pastry to a thickness of about 3mm/⅛in and line a 23cm/9in pie dish.

3 Roll out the smaller piece of pastry to a round slightly larger than the top of the pie. Support it on the prepared baking sheet, then stamp out four hearts from the centre of the pastry, using a cutter. Reserve the pastry hearts.

4 Make the filling by mixing all the ingredients in a bowl. Use the larger quantity of sugar if the plums are very tart. Spoon the filling into the pastry case, then lift the pastry on the greaseproof paper and slide it into position over the filling. Trim and pinch to seal. Arrange the cut-out pastry hearts on top. Glaze the top of the pie with milk and bake for 15 minutes. Lower the oven temperature to 180°C/350°F/Gas 4 and bake for 30–35 minutes more, protecting the top with foil if needed.

92

Walnut & Pear Lattice Pie

INGREDIENTS

225g/8oz/2 cups plain flour
1.5ml/¼ tsp salt
115g/4oz/½ cup chilled butter, diced
25g/1oz/¼ cup finely chopped walnuts
45-60ml/3-4 tbsp iced water
50g/2oz/⅓ cup icing sugar
15ml/1 tbsp lemon juice
FILLING
900g/2lb pears
50g/2oz/¼ cup caster sugar
60ml/4 tbsp plain flour
2.5ml/½ tsp grated lemon rind
45ml/3 tbsp raisins or sultanas
45ml/3 tbsp chopped walnuts
2.5ml/½ tsp ground cinnamon

SERVES 6–8

1 Sift the flour and salt together into a mixing bowl. Rub in the butter and stir in the walnuts and enough iced water to moisten. Gather into a ball, wrap and chill for 30 minutes. Preheat the oven to 190°C/375°F/Gas 5.

2 Make the filling. Peel the pears and slice into a bowl. Add the caster sugar, flour and rind. Toss to coat the fruit. Add the raisins or sultanas, walnuts and cinnamon. Mix lightly.

3 Roll out half the pastry on a lightly floured surface and line a 23cm/9in pie tin that is about 5cm/2in deep. Roll out the remaining pastry to a 28cm/11in round and cut it into 1cm/½in wide strips. Spoon the filling into the pastry case. Arrange the pastry strips on top, carefully weaving them in and out to make a lattice. Bake for about 55 minutes or until golden.

4 Combine the icing sugar, lemon juice and 5–10ml/1–2 tsp cold water in a bowl. Mix until smooth. Remove the pie from the oven, drizzle over the icing then leave to cool slightly before serving.

Pumpkin Pie

INGREDIENTS

25g / 1oz / ¼ cup pecan nuts, chopped
500g / 1¼lb / 2 cups pumpkin purée
475ml / 16fl oz / 2 cups single cream
175g / 6oz / ¾ cup light brown sugar
1.5ml / ¼ tsp salt
5ml / 1 tsp ground cinnamon
2.5ml / ½ tsp ground ginger
1.5ml / ½ tsp ground cloves
3.75ml / ¾ tsp grated nutmeg
2 eggs
PASTRY
200g / 7oz / 1¾ cups plain flour
2.5ml / ½ tsp salt
115g / 4oz / ½ cup butter
10-15ml / 2-3 tbsp iced water

SERVES 8

1 Preheat the oven to 220°C/425°F/ Gas 7 and sift the flour and salt into a bowl. Cut in the butter, then add just enough iced water to make a firm dough.

2 On a lightly floured surface, roll out the dough to 5mm/¼in thickness. Use it to line a 23cm/9in pie dish. Trim off the excess dough.

3 Use the dough trimmings to make a decorative rope edge: cut the dough into strips and twist together in pairs. Dampen the rim of the pie shell and press on the rope edge. Sprinkle the chopped pecans over the bottom of the pie shell.

4 With an electric mixer, beat together the pumpkin purée, cream, brown sugar, salt, spices and eggs and pour the pumpkin mixture into the pie shell. Bake for 10 minutes, then reduce the heat to 180°C/350°F/Gas 4 and continue baking for about 45 minutes until the filling is set. Let the pie cool in the dish, set on a wire rack.

Open Apple Pie

INGREDIENTS

275g/10oz/2½ cups plain flour
2.5ml/½ tsp salt
115g/4oz/½ cup chilled unsalted
butter, diced
50g/2oz/¼ cup chilled vegetable fat, diced
75-90ml/5-6 tbsp iced water
FILLING
1.5kg/3lb sweet-tart firm eating or
cooking apples
50g/2oz/¼ cup sugar
10ml/2 tsp ground cinnamon
grated rind and juice of 1 lemon
25g/1oz/2 tbsp butter, diced
30-45ml/2-3 tbsp clear honey

SERVES 8

1 Sift the flour and salt together into a mixing bowl. Rub in the butter and vegetable fat until the mixture resembles coarse breadcrumbs. Stir in just enough iced water to moisten the dry ingredients, then gather together to make a ball. Wrap the pastry and chill for 30 minutes.

2 Preheat the oven to 200°C/400°F/Gas 6. Very lightly grease a deep 23cm/9in pie dish and set aside. Peel, quarter and core the apples, then slice them into a bowl. Add the sugar, cinnamon, lemon rind and juice and toss together well.

3 Roll out the pastry on a lightly floured surface to a 30cm/12in round. Place the pastry over the pie dish so that the excess dough overhangs the edges. Fill with the apple mixture, then fold in the pastry edges, crimping them loosely to make a decorative border. Dot the apples with the diced butter.

4 Bake the pie for about 45 minutes, until the pastry is golden and the apples are tender. Melt the honey in a saucepan. Remove the pie from the oven and immediately brush the honey over the apples to glaze. Serve warm or at room temperature.

95

Chocolate Cheesecake Pie

INGREDIENTS

350g / 12oz / 1½ cups cream cheese, softened
60ml / 4 tbsp double cream
225g / 8oz / 1 cup caster sugar
50g / 2oz / ½ cup cocoa powder
2.5ml / ½ tsp ground cinnamon
3 eggs
BASE
75g / 3oz sweetmeal biscuits, crushed
45g / 1½oz amaretti (or extra sweetmeal biscuits), crushed
75g / 3oz / ⅓ cup unsalted butter, melted
DECORATION
whipped cream
chocolate curls

SERVES 8

1 Preheat the oven to 180°C/350°F/Gas 4. Make the base by mixing the crushed biscuits with the melted butter. Press the mixture evenly over the bottom and sides of a 23cm/9in pie dish. Bake for 8 minutes, then cool. Leave the oven on, and put a baking sheet inside to heat.

2 Beat the cheese and cream in a bowl with an electric mixer until smooth. Beat in the sugar, cocoa and cinnamon until blended, then add the eggs, one at a

time, beating for just long enough to combine. Pour the filling into the biscuit case and bake on the hot baking sheet for 25–30 minutes. The filling will sink as the cheesecake cools. Decorate with whipped cream and chocolate curls when cold.

Maple Pecan Pie

INGREDIENTS

115g/4oz/1 cup pecan halves
3 eggs, beaten
115g/4oz/½ cup dark brown sugar
150ml/¼ pint/⅔ cup golden syrup
75ml/3fl oz/6 tbsp maple syrup
2.5ml/½ tsp vanilla essence
3.75ml/¾ tsp salt
PASTRY
165g/5½oz/1⅓ cups plain flour
2.5ml/½ tsp salt
5ml/1 tsp ground cinnamon
115g/4oz/½ cup butter
30-45ml/2-3 tbsp iced water

SERVES 8

97

1 Preheat the oven to 220°C/425°F/Gas 7. Make the pastry. Sift the flour, salt and cinnamon into a mixing bowl. Rub in the butter until the mixture resembles coarse crumbs. Sprinkle in the iced water, 15ml/1 tbsp at a time, tossing lightly with your fingertips or a fork, until the dough clumps together and will form a ball.

2 On a lightly floured surface, roll out the dough to a circle 30cm/12in in diameter. Use it to line a 23cm/9in pie dish, easing in the dough and being careful not to stretch it. Make a fluted edge.

3 Using a fork, prick the bottom and sides of the pie shell all over. Bake for 10–15 minutes, until lightly browned. Cool, then sprinkle the pecans over the bottom of the shell. Reduce the oven temperature to 180°C/350°F/Gas 4.

4 Beat the eggs, sugar, syrups, vanilla essence and salt in a bowl. Pour over the pecans. Bake for about 40 minutes. Cool in the dish, on a wire rack.

Cherry Lattice Pie

INGREDIENTS

2 x 450g/1lb cans cherries, drained or
900g/2lb/4 cups pitted fresh cherries
75g/3oz/6 tbsp caster sugar
25g/1oz/¼ cup plain flour
25ml/1½ tbsp fresh lemon juice
1.5ml/¼ tsp almond essence
25g/1oz/2 tbsp butter or margarine
PASTRY
225g/8oz/2 cups plain flour
5ml/1 tsp salt
175g/6oz/¾ cup butter or margarine, diced
60-75ml/4-5 tbsp iced water

SERVES 8

1 Make the pastry. Sift the flour and salt into a mixing bowl. Rub in the butter or margarine until the mixture resembles coarse breadcrumbs. Sprinkle in the iced water, 15ml/1 tbsp at a time, tossing with your fingertips until the dough forms a ball.

2 Divide the dough in half and shape each half into a ball. On a lightly floured surface, roll out one of the balls to a circle about 30cm/12in in diameter.

3 Use the dough circle to line a 23cm/9in pie dish, easing the dough in and being careful not to stretch it. Trim off all the excess dough, leaving a 1cm/½in overhang around the rim. Roll out the remaining dough to 3mm/⅛in thickness. With a sharp knife, cut out 11 strips, 1cm/½in wide.

4 In a mixing bowl, combine the cherries, sugar, flour, lemon juice and almond essence. Spoon the mixture into the pastry shell and dot the butter or margarine over the surface.

5 For the lattice, space five of the pastry strips over the cherry filling and fold every other strip back. Lay a strip across, perpendicular to the others. Fold  the strips back over the filling. Continue in this way, folding back every other strip each time you add a cross strip. Trim the ends of the lattice strips to make them even with the pastry overhang. Press together so that the edge rests on the pie dish rim. Flute the edge. Chill for 15 minutes. Preheat the oven to 220°C/425°F/Gas 7.

6 Bake the pie for 30 minutes, covering the edge with foil, if necessary, to prevent burning.

Peach Leaf Pie

INGREDIENTS

1.2kg/2½lb ripe peaches, peeled and sliced
juice of 1 lemon
90g/3½oz/½ cup caster sugar
45ml/3 tbsp cornflour
1.5ml/¼ tsp grated nutmeg
2.5ml/½ tsp ground cinnamon
1 egg beaten with 1 tbsp water, to glaze
25g/1oz/2 tbsp butter, diced
cream or ice cream, to serve
PASTRY
225g/8oz/2 cups plain flour
2.5ml/¾ tsp salt
150g/5oz/⅔ cup cold butter, cut in pieces
5-6 tbsp iced water

SERVES 8

1 Sift the flour and salt into a bowl. Rub in the butter, then stir in just enough iced water to bind the dough. Gather into two balls, one slightly larger than the other. Wrap and chill for at least 20 minutes. Preheat the oven to 220°C/425°F/Gas 7.

2 Combine the peaches with the lemon juice, sugar, cornflour and spices. Set aside.

3 Roll out the larger dough ball thinly and line a 23cm/9in pie dish. Roll out the remaining dough. Cut out 7.5cm/3in leaves. Mark with veins.

4 Brush the bottom of the pie shell with egg glaze. Add the peaches, piling them higher in the centre. Dot with the butter. Starting from the rim, cover the

peaches with concentric rings of leaves. Place tiny balls of dough in the centre, if you like. Brush with the glaze. Bake for 10 minutes. Lower the heat to 180°C/350°F/Gas 4 and bake for 35–40 minutes more. Serve hot or cold, with cream or ice cream.

Lemon Meringue Pie

INGREDIENTS

275g/10oz/1¼ cups caster sugar
25g/1oz/2 tbsp cornflour
pinch of salt
10ml/2 tsp finely grated lemon rind
120ml/4fl oz/½ cup fresh lemon juice
250ml/8fl oz/1 cup water
3 eggs, separated
45g/1½oz/3 tbsp butter
23cm/9in pastry case, made from rich shortcrust pastry baked blind

SERVES 6

1 Combine 200g/7oz/1 cup sugar, the cornflour, salt and lemon rind in a saucepan. Stir in the lemon juice and water until smoothly blended. Bring to the boil over moderately high heat, stirring all the time. Simmer for 1 minute or until thickened.

2 Blend in the egg yolks. Cook over low heat for a further 2 minutes, stirring constantly. Remove from the heat. Add the butter and mix well.

3 Pour the lemon filling into the pastry case. Spread it evenly and level the surface. Cover closely and leave to cool completely. Preheat the oven to 180°C/350°F/Gas 4.

4 Whisk the egg whites to soft peaks. Add the rest of the sugar and continue whisking until the meringue is stiff and glossy.

5 Swirl the stiff meringue over the filling, sealing it to the rim of the pastry case. Bake for 10–15 minutes, until the meringue is golden. Serve the pie cold.

Pear & Blueberry Pie

INGREDIENTS

675g / 1½lb / 6 cups blueberries
30ml / 2 tbsp caster sugar
15ml / 1 tbsp arrowroot
2 ripe but firm pears, peeled, cored and sliced
2.5ml / ½ tsp ground cinnamon
grated rind of ½ lemon
beaten egg, to glaze
caster sugar, for sprinkling
crème fraîche, to serve
PASTRY
225g / 8oz / 2 cups plain flour
pinch of salt
50g / 2oz / 4 tbsp lard, cubed
50g / 2oz / 4 tbsp butter, cubed

SERVES 4

1 Make the pastry. Sift the flour and salt into a bowl and rub in the fats. Stir in 45ml/3 tbsp cold water and mix to a dough. Chill for 30 minutes.

2 Place 225g/8oz/2 cups of the blueberries in a pan with the sugar. Cover and cook gently until the blueberries have softened. Press through a sieve.

3 Blend the arrowroot with 30ml/2 tbsp cold water and add to the blueberry purée. Place in a small saucepan and bring to the boil, stirring until thickened. Cool the mixture slightly.

4 Place a baking sheet in the oven and preheat to 190°C/375°F/ Gas 5. Roll out just over half the pastry on a lightly floured surface and use to line a 20cm/8in shallow pie dish or plate; do this by lopping the pastry over the rolling pin and lifting into position.

5 Mix together the remaining blueberries, the pears, cinnamon and lemon rind and spoon into the dish. Pour the blueberry purée over the top.

6 Roll out the remaining pastry to just larger than the pie dish and lay over the filling. Press the edges together to seal, then trim off any excess pastry and crimp the edge. Make a small slit in the centre to allow steam to escape. Brush with egg and sprinkle with caster sugar. Bake the pie on the hot baking sheet for 40–45 minutes, until golden. Serve warm with crème fraîche.

Mince Pies with Orange & Cinnamon Pastry

INGREDIENTS

225g / 8oz / 1¼ cups mincemeat
beaten egg, to glaze
icing sugar, for dusting
PASTRY
225g / 8oz / 2 cups plain flour
25g / 1oz / ¼ cup icing sugar
10ml / 2 tsp ground cinnamon
175g / 6oz / ¾ cup butter
grated rind of 1 orange
about 60ml / 4 tbsp iced water

MAKES 18

1 Sift together the flour, icing sugar and cinnamon, then rub in the butter until the mixture resembles breadcrumbs. (Pulse in a food processor, if you like.) Stir in the grated orange rind. Mix to a firm dough with the iced water. Knead lightly, then roll out to a 5mm/¼in thickness. Using a 6cm/2½in round fluted cutter, stamp out 18 circles, re-rolling the dough as necessary.

2 Using a 5cm/2in round fluted cutter, stamp out 18 smaller circles.

3 Line two muffin tins with the 18 larger circles. Place a small spoonful of mincemeat into each pastry case and top with the smaller pastry circles, pressing the edges lightly together to seal in the filling. Cut a small steam vent in the top of each pie.

4 Glaze the tops of the pies with egg and leave to rest in the fridge for 30 minutes. Preheat the oven to 200°C/400°F/Gas 6.

5 Bake the pies for 15–20 minutes, until they are golden brown. Remove them to wire racks to cool. Dust with icing sugar before serving.

104

Blueberry Pie

INGREDIENTS

225g / 8oz / 2 cups flour quantity short-crust pastry
575g / 1¼lb / 5 cups blueberries
*175g / 6oz / ¾ cup caster sugar,
plus extra for sprinkling*
45ml / 3 tbsp plain flour
5ml / 1 tsp grated orange rind
1.5ml / ¼ tsp grated nutmeg
30ml / 2 tbsp orange juice
5ml / 1 tsp lemon juice

SERVES 6–8

1 Preheat the oven to 190°C/375°F/Gas 5. Roll out half of the pastry and use to line a 23cm/9in pie tin that is about 5cm/2in deep.

2 Combine the blueberries, sugar, plain flour, grated orange rind and nutmeg in a bowl. Toss the mixture gently to coat all the fruit evenly. Tip the blueberry mixture into the pastry case and spread it evenly. Sprinkle over the citrus juices.

3 Roll out the remaining pastry and cover the pie. Cut out heart shapes, or cut two slits for releasing steam. Cut out small hearts from the trimmings to

decorate the pie and finish the edge with a twisted pastry strip. Brush the top lightly with water and then sprinkle evenly with about 30ml/2 tbsp caster sugar.

4 Bake the pie for about 45 minutes, or until the pastry is golden brown. Serve warm or cold.

Tarts, Gâteaux & Cakes

From the elegant Raspberry & Hazelnut Meringue Cake to the extravagant White Chocolate & Strawberry Gâteaux, for a truly memorable occasion indulge yourself in this sensational collection of stunning desserts.

Chocolate Apricot Linzer Tart

INGREDIENTS

350g/12oz/2 cups ready-to-eat
dried apricots
120ml/4fl oz/½ cup orange juice
175ml/6fl oz/¾ cup water
45ml/3 tbsp granulated sugar
45ml/3 tbsp apricot jam
2.5ml/½ tsp ground cinnamon
2.5ml/½ tsp almond essence
75g/3oz/½ cup chocolate chips
icing sugar, for dusting
PASTRY
50g/2oz/½ cup whole blanched almonds
115g/4oz/½ cup caster sugar
215g/7½oz/scant 2 cups plain flour
30ml/2 tbsp cocoa powder
5ml/1 tsp ground cinnamon
2.5ml/½ tsp salt
5ml/1 tsp grated orange rind
225g/8oz/1 cup butter, diced
30-45ml/2-3 tbsp iced water

SERVES 10–12

1 Mix the apricots, orange juice and water in a large pan. Bring to the boil, and simmer them for 15–20 minutes, until the liquid is absorbed, stirring frequently to prevent sticking. Stir in the sugar, jam, cinnamon and almond essence, then purée in a food processor or press through a sieve.

2 Make the pastry. Process the almonds with half the sugar in the food processor, until finely ground. Sift the flour, cocoa, cinnamon and salt. Add to the processor with the remaining sugar and process to mix, then add the rind and butter and process for about 15 seconds, until mixture resembles coarse crumbs. Pulse, adding just enough iced water to make the chocolate dough stick together.

3 Knead the dough lightly. With floured fingers, press half the dough on to the bottom and sides of a 28cm/11in springform flan tin. Prick the base with a fork, then chill the pie shell. Roll out the remaining dough between two sheets of clear film to a 28cm/11in round; chill for about 30 minutes. Preheat the oven to 180°C/350°F/Gas 4.

4 Spread filling in the pie shell and sprinkle with the chocolate chips. Cut the dough round into strips and arrange a lattice over the filling. Bake for 35–40  minutes, or until top of pastry is set and the filling bubbles. Cool slightly and remove the sides of the tin. Lay strips of paper across the lattice and dust with icing sugar. Remove the paper carefully and slide the pie on to a serving plate.

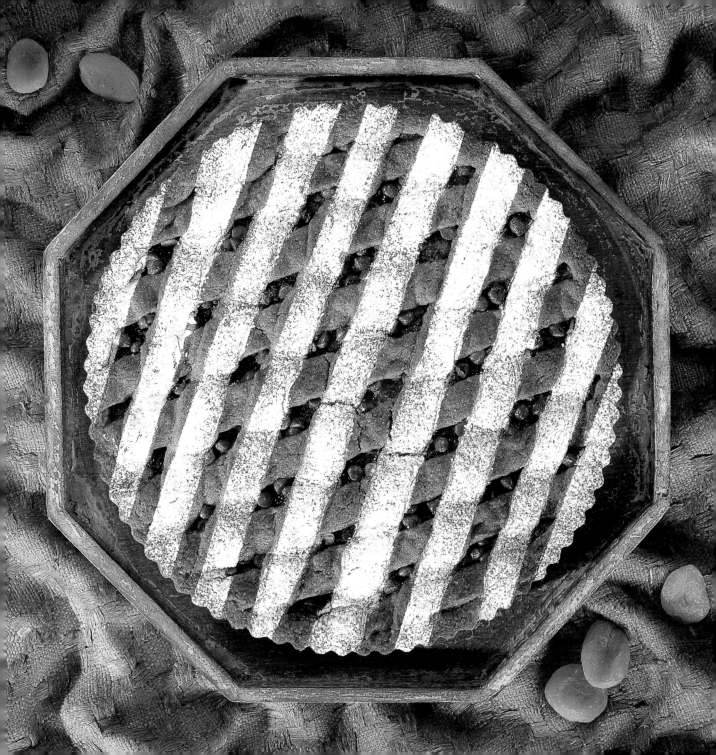

Red Berry Tart with Lemon Cream Filling

INGREDIENTS

150g / 5oz / 1¼ cups plain flour
25g / 1oz / ¼ cup cornflour
45ml / 3 tbsp icing sugar
90g / 3½oz / scant ½ cup chilled unsalted
butter, diced
2 egg yolks
5ml / 1 tsp vanilla essence
sprig of mint, to decorate
FILLING
200g / 7oz / scant 1 cup cream cheese, softened
45ml / 3 tbsp lemon curd
grated rind and juice of 1 lemon
icing sugar (see method)
225g / 8oz / 2 cups mixed red berry fruits
45ml / 3 tbsp redcurrant jelly

SERVES 6—8

1 Sift the flour, cornflour and icing sugar into a bowl. Rub in the butter until the mixture resembles breadcrumbs. (This can be done in a food processor). Beat the egg yolks with the vanilla essence in a cup. Add to the dry ingredients and mix to a firm dough, adding a little cold water if necessary.

2 Roll the pastry out into a round and use to line a 23cm/9in flan tin, pressing the pastry well up the sides after trimming. Prick the base all over with a fork. Chill for 30 minutes. Line the pastry case with greaseproof paper and fill with baking beans.

3 Preheat the oven to 200°C/400°F/Gas 6. Place the pastry case on a baking sheet and bake for 20 minutes, removing the paper and beans for the last 5 minutes. Cool, then remove the pastry case from the tin and place on a serving plate.

4 Cream together the cheese, lemon curd, lemon rind and lemon juice, adding icing sugar to sweeten, if liked. Spread the mixture in the pastry case and then arrange the mixed berries on top. Warm the redcurrant jelly in a saucepan, sieve it, then trickle or brush it over the fruit. Decorate the tart with a sprig of mint and serve at once.

Hazelnut Meringue Torte with Pears

INGREDIENTS

175g/6oz/¾ cup granulated sugar
1 vanilla pod, split
475ml/16fl oz/2 cups water
4 ripe pears, peeled, halved and cored
6 egg whites
275g/10oz/2½ cups icing sugar
175g/6oz/1¼ cups ground hazelnuts
5ml/1 tsp vanilla essence
50g/2oz plain chocolate, melted
chocolate caraque, to decorate
CHOCOLATE CREAM
475ml/16fl oz/2 cups whipping cream
275g/10oz plain chocolate, melted
60ml/4 tbsp hazelnut-flavour liqueur

SERVES 8–10

1 In a pan large enough to hold the pears in a single layer, combine the sugar, vanilla pod and water. Bring to the boil, stirring until the sugar dissolves. Reduce the heat and add the pears. Cover and simmer for 12–15 minutes until tender. Remove from heat and leave to cool. Preheat the oven to 180°C/350°F/Gas 4.

2 Draw a 23cm/9in circle on two sheets of non-stick baking paper and place on two baking sheets.

3 Whisk the egg whites until soft peaks form then gradually add the icing sugar, whisking until stiff and glossy. Gently fold in the nuts and vanilla and spoon  the meringue on to the marked circles. Bake for 1 hour. Turn off the heat and cool in the oven.

4 Slice the pear halves lengthways. Make the chocolate cream. Beat the cream to soft peaks, then fold in the melted chocolate and liqueur. Put a third of the chocolate cream into an icing bag fitted with a star tip. Spread one meringue layer with half the remaining chocolate cream and top with half the pears. Pipe rosettes around the edge.

5 Top with the second meringue and the remaining chocolate cream and pear slices. Pipe rosettes around the edge. Drizzle the melted chocolate over the pears and decorate with the chocolate caraque. Chill for 1 hour before serving.

Raspberry & Hazelnut Meringue Cake

INGREDIENTS

4 egg whites
225g/8oz/1 cup caster sugar
few drops of vanilla essence
5ml/1 tsp malt vinegar
115g/4oz/1 cup roasted chopped
hazelnuts, ground
300ml/½ pint/1¼ cups double cream
350g/12 oz/3 cups raspberries
icing sugar, for dusting
mint sprigs, to decorate
SAUCE
225g/8oz/2 cups raspberries
45-60ml/3-4 tbsp icing sugar
15ml/1 tbsp orange liqueur

SERVES 6

1 Preheat the oven to 180°C/350°F/ Gas 4. Base-line and grease two 20cm/8in sandwich cake tins. Whisk the egg whites in a bowl until stiff peaks  form. Gradually whisk in the caster sugar. When stiff, gently fold in the vanilla, vinegar and nuts.

2 Divide the mixture between the prepared tins and bake for 50–60 minutes, or until crisp. Remove gently from the tins and leave to cool on a wire rack.

3 Make the sauce. Purée the raspberries with the icing sugar and liqueur in a food processor or blender. Press through a fine sieve into a jug. Chill until ready to serve.

4 In a bowl, whip the cream to soft peaks. Gently fold in the raspberries. Place one round of meringue on a serving plate and spread the raspberry and cream  mixture evenly over the top. Place the second round of meringue on top to form a sandwich.

5 Dust the top of the gâteau liberally with icing sugar and decorate with mint sprigs. Serve with the raspberry sauce. (To cut the gâteau, use a large and very sharp knife.)

Chocolate Pavlova with Chocolate Curls

INGREDIENTS

275g/10oz/2½ cups icing sugar
15ml/1 tbsp unsweetened cocoa
5ml/1 tsp cornflour
5 egg whites, at room temperature
pinch of salt
5ml/1 tsp cider vinegar or lemon juice
CHOCOLATE CREAM
175g/6oz plain chocolate, chopped
120ml/4fl oz/½ cup milk
25g/1oz/2 tbsp butter, diced
30ml/2 tbsp brandy
475ml/16fl oz/2 cups double cream
TOPPING
450g/1lb/4 cups mixed berries or diced
mango, papaya, lychees and pineapple
chocolate curls
icing sugar

SERVES 8–10

1 Preheat the oven to 160°C/325°F/Gas 3. Place a sheet of non-stick baking paper on to a baking sheet and mark a 20cm/8in circle on it. Sift 45ml/3 tbsp of the icing sugar with the cocoa and cornflour and set aside. Using an electric mixer, beat the egg whites until frothy. Add the salt and beat until the whites form stiff peaks.

2 Sprinkle the remaining icing sugar into the egg whites, a little at a time, making sure each addition is dissolved before beating in the next. Fold in the cornflour mixture, then quickly fold in the vinegar or lemon juice.

3 Now spoon the mixture on to the paper circle, with the sides higher than the centre. Bake for 1 hour, until set, then turn off the oven but leave the meringue inside for 1 hour longer. Remove from the oven, peel off the paper and leave to cool.

4 Make the chocolate cream. Melt the chocolate and milk over a low heat, stirring until smooth. Remove from the heat and whisk in the butter and brandy. Cool for 1 hour.

5 Transfer the meringue to a serving plate. When the chocolate mixture has cooled, but is not too firm, beat the cream until soft peaks form. Stir half the cream into the chocolate mixture to lighten it, then fold in the remaining cream. Spoon it into the centre of the meringue. Arrange fruit and chocolate curls in the centre of the meringue, over the cream. Dust with icing sugar.

Chocolate Fudge Gâteau

INGREDIENTS

225g/8oz plain chocolate, chopped
115g/4oz/½ cup unsalted butter, diced
150ml/¼ pint/⅔ cup water
225g/8oz/1 cup caster sugar
10ml/2 tsp vanilla essence
2 eggs, separated
150ml/¼ pint/⅔ cup soured cream
275g/10oz/2½ cups plain flour
10ml/2 tsp baking powder
5ml/1 tsp bicarbonate of soda
pinch of cream of tartar
chocolate curls, raspberries and icing sugar,
to decorate
CHOCOLATE FUDGE FILLING
450g/1lb plain chocolate, chopped
225g/8oz/1 cup unsalted butter
75ml/5 tbsp brandy
225g/8oz/¾ cup seedless raspberry preserve
GANACHE
250ml/8fl oz/1 cup double cream
225g/8oz plain chocolate, chopped
30ml/2 tbsp brandy

SERVES 18–20

1 Preheat the oven to 180°C/350°F/Gas 4. Base-line and grease a 25cm/10in springform cake tin. Place the chocolate, butter and water in a saucepan. Heat gently, until melted.

2 Pour into a large bowl and beat in the sugar and vanilla essence. Leave to cool, then beat in the egg yolks. Fold in the soured cream. Sift the dry ingredients then fold them into the mixture. Whisk the egg whites in a bowl until stiff and gently fold in.

3 Pour the mixture into the prepared tin. Bake for 45–50 minutes. Leave to cool for 10 minutes then remove from the tin, place on a wire rack and leave to cool completely. Wash and dry the tin.

4 Make the fudge filling. Gently melt the chocolate and butter with 60ml/4 tbsp of brandy. Set aside to cool. Meanwhile, cut the cake into three layers. Heat the preserve with the remaining brandy and spread over each cake layer. Leave to set.

5 Return the bottom layer to the tin, spread with half the filling, top with the middle cake layer and spread over the remaining filling. Add the top cake layer and press down gently. Chill overnight.

6 Make the ganache. Bring the cream to the boil, remove from the heat and stir in the chocolate, then the brandy. Strain, then set aside for 5 minutes to thicken. Remove the cake from its tin and pour the ganache over the top, smoothing down over the sides to cover. Pipe any remaining ganache around the base of the cake using a star-shaped nozzle. When set, decorate with chocolate curls, raspberries and icing sugar. Do not chill the glazed cake.

White Chocolate & Strawberry Gâteau

INGREDIENTS

115g/4oz fine quality white chocolate, chopped
120ml/4fl oz/½ cup double cream
120ml/4fl oz/½ cup milk
15ml/1 tbsp rum or vanilla essence
115g/4oz/½ cup unsalted butter, softened
175g/6oz/¾ cup caster sugar
3 eggs
225g/8oz/2 cups plain flour
5ml/1 tsp baking powder
pinch of salt
675g/1½lb/6 cups strawberries, sliced,
plus extra for decorating
750ml/1¼ pints/3 cups whipping cream
30ml/2 tbsp rum
WHITE CHOCOLATE MOUSSE FILLING
250g/9oz fine quality white chocolate, chopped
350ml/12fl oz/1½ cups whipping or
double cream
30ml/2 tbsp rum

SERVES 10

1 Preheat the oven to 180°C/350°F/Gas 4. Grease and flour two 23cm/9in round cake tins, about 5cm/2in deep. Base-line the tins with non-stick baking paper. Melt the chocolate in the cream in a double boiler over low heat, stirring until smooth. Stir in the milk and rum or vanilla essence. Set aside to cool.

2 Cream the butter and sugar until fluffy. Beat in the eggs one at a time. Sift together the flour, baking powder and salt and add to the egg mixture in batches, alternately with the melted chocolate, until just blended.

3 Divide the mixture between the prepared tins. Bake for 20–25 minutes or until a skewer inserted in the centre of each cake layer comes out clean. Cool in the tins for 10 minutes, then turn out on to wire racks, peel off the baking paper and leave to cool completely.

4 Make the filling. Melt the chocolate with the cream in a saucepan over low heat, stirring frequently. Stir in the rum and pour into a bowl. Chill until just set, then whip the mixture lightly until it has a mousse-like consistency.

5 Slice each cake layer in half horizontally to make four layers. Spread a third of the mousse on top of one layer and arrange a third of the strawberries over the mousse. Place another cake layer on top of the first and cover with mousse and strawberries as before. Repeat this process once more, then top with the final cake layer.

6 Whip the cream with the rum. Spread about half the flavoured cream over the top and sides of the cake. Use the remaining cream and strawberries to decorate the cake as desired.

Orange & Apricot Roulade

INGREDIENTS

4 egg whites
115g/4oz/½ cup golden caster sugar
50g/2oz/½ cup plain flour
finely grated rind of 1 small orange
45ml/3 tbsp orange juice
icing sugar, for dusting
shreds of pared orange rind, to decorate
FILLING
115g/4oz/⅔ cup ready-to-eat dried apricots
150ml/¼ pint/⅔ cup orange juice

SERVES 6

1 Preheat the oven to 200°C/400°F/Gas 6. Grease a 33 x 23cm/13 x 9in Swiss roll tin and line it with non-stick baking paper. Grease the paper. Whisk the egg whites in a grease-free bowl until soft peaks form. Gradually add the sugar, whisking hard after each addition, then gently fold in the flour, orange rind and juice.

2 Spoon the mixture into the prepared Swiss roll tin and spread it evenly. Bake for 15–18 minutes, or until the sponge is firm and pale golden in colour.

Turn out on to a sheet of non-stick baking paper. Working quickly, roll up the sponge loosely from one short side and leave the roll to cool.

3 Make the filling. Roughly chop the apricots and place them in a saucepan with the orange juice. Bring to simmering point, cover and cook until most of the liquid has been absorbed. Purée the apricots in a food processor or blender. Cool.

4 Carefully unroll the roulade and spread evenly with the apricot purée. Roll up again and transfer to a platter. Arrange paper strips diagonally across the roll,

sprinkle it lightly with icing sugar, then carefully remove the paper to create the patterned effect. Decorate the roll with orange rind and serve.

Chocolate & Mint Fudge Cake

INGREDIENTS

6-10 mint leaves
175g/6oz/¾ cup caster sugar
115g/4oz/½ cup butter, plus extra
for greasing
75g/3oz/½ cup freshly made mashed potato
50g/2oz plain chocolate, melted
175g/6oz/1½ cups self-raising flour
pinch of salt
2 eggs, beaten

FILLING
4 mint leaves
115g/4oz/½ cup butter
115g/4oz/¾ cup icing sugar
30ml/2 tbsp chocolate mint liqueur

FUDGE TOPPING
225g/8oz/1 cup butter
50g/2oz/¼ cup granulated sugar
30ml/2 tbsp chocolate mint liqueur
30ml/2 tbsp water
175g/6oz/1¼ cups icing sugar
25g/1oz/¼ cup cocoa powder
pecan nut halves, to decorate

SERVES 8–10

1 Tear the mint leaves into pieces and mix in a bowl with the caster sugar. Leave overnight.

2 Preheat the oven to 200°C/400°F/Gas 6. Grease and line a 20cm/8in cake tin. Sift the mint-flavoured caster sugar, discarding the mint leaves. Cream the butter and mint-flavoured sugar with the mashed potato, then add the melted chocolate. Sift in half the flour with the salt, and add half the beaten eggs. Mix well, then add the remaining flour and eggs to the mixture.

3 Spoon the mixture into the prepared cake tin. Bake for 25–30 minutes or until a skewer inserted in the cake comes out clean. Turn the cake out on a wire rack to cool. When cool, split it into two layers.

4 Make the filling. Chop the mint leaves finely. Cream the butter, then mix in the icing sugar and mint leaves to give a smooth buttercream. Sprinkle the liqueur over both layers of the cake, then sand-wich them together with the filling.

5 Make the topping. Mix the butter, granulated sugar, liqueur and water in a small saucepan. Heat until the butter and sugar have melted, then boil the mixture for 5 minutes. Sift the icing sugar and cocoa into a large mixing bowl and add the hot but-ter and liqueur mixture. Beat with a large spoon, until cool and thick. Cover the cake with the fudge topping and decorate with the pecan nut halves.

French Chocolate Cake

INGREDIENTS

225g/8oz/1 cup unsalted butter,
cut into pieces
250g/9oz plain chocolate, chopped
115g/4oz/½ cup granulated sugar
30ml/2 tbsp brandy or orange-flavour liqueur
5 eggs
15ml/1 tbsp plain flour
icing sugar, to decorate
sour cream and cherries, to serve

SERVES 10

1 Preheat the oven to 180°C/350°F/Gas 4. Base-line and grease a 23 x 5cm/9 x 2in springform tin. Wrap foil around the tin so it is water-tight.

2 Stir the butter, the chocolate and sugar over a low heat until smooth. Cool slightly. Stir in the liqueur. In a mixing bowl, beat the eggs lightly, then beat in the flour. Slowly beat in the chocolate mixture until blended. Pour into the tin, smoothing the surface.

3 Place the springform tin in a roasting tin and pour in boiling water to come 2cm/¾in up the side of the springform tin. Bake for 25–30 minutes until the edge of the cake is set, but the centre is still soft. Remove the foil. Cool in the tin on a wire rack (the cake will sink and may crack).

4 Turn the cake on to a wire rack. Remove the springform tin bottom and paper, so the bottom of the cake is now the top.

5 Cut 6–8 strips of non-stick baking paper 2.5cm/1in wide and place them randomly over the cake, or make a lattice-style pattern if you wish. Dust the cake with icing sugar, then carefully remove the paper. Slide the cake on to a serving plate and serve with sour cream and fresh cherries.

Index